GRACE IN A TREE STUMP

To Rick,
  A gracious friend who
extends kindness + thought.
fulness to those whose lives
you touch. Happy Birthday!
                    Barb

Other books by J. Ellsworth Kalas
from Westminster John Knox Press

Preaching the Calendar: Celebrating Holidays and Holy Days

GRACE IN A TREE STUMP
Old Testament Stories of God's Love

J. Ellsworth Kalas

WESTMINSTER
JOHN KNOX PRESS
LOUISVILLE · KENTUCKY

Book design by Sharon Adams
Cover design by Eric Walljasper, Minneapolis, MN

First edition
Published by Westminster John Knox Press
Louisville, Kentucky

This book is printed on acid-free paper that meets the American National Standards Institute Z39.48 standard. ∞

PRINTED IN THE UNITED STATES OF AMERICA

05 06 07 08 09 10 11 12 13 14—10 9 8 7 6 5 4 3 2

Library of Congress Cataloging-in-Publication Data

Kalas, J. Ellsworth.
    Grace in a tree stump : Old Testament stories of God's love / J. Ellsworth Kalas.
        p. cm.
    Includes bibliographical references.
    ISBN-13: 978-0-664-22900-9 (alk. paper)
    ISBN-10: 0-664-22900-X (alk. paper)
    1. Grace—Biblical teaching. 2. God—Love. 3. Bible stories, English.
    4. Bible. O.T.—Criticism, interpretation, etc. I. Title.

BS1199.G68K35   2005
234—dc22   2004057206

Contents

Chapter 1

Grace in the Morning

Scripture Lesson: Genesis 1:1–5, 26–31

*T*heologians aren't usually good at shorthand. They're better at expounding on a line from the Creed or a verse from the Scriptures until it becomes a book—or still better, a series of books. Nevertheless, they've done pretty well at defining *grace* with brevity. *"Unmerited favor"* is the definition one is most likely to hear. This is succinct, but sufficient. Grace is unmerited favor.

If grace is unmerited favor, it gets into the biblical story very early. In the first chapter of Genesis, to be specific.

You remember the story: "In the beginning when God created the heavens and the earth, the earth was a formless void and darkness covered the face of the deep, while a wind from God swept over the face of the waters" (Gen. 1:1–2)—or as another translation puts it, "the spirit of God hovered over the face of the waters."[1] Early in the creation, God apparently had a formless, roiling mass, enveloped in darkness. The only redeeming feature, it seems, is that the Spirit of God was brooding over this mass, as if anticipating what might become of it.

Then God set about the process of converting this mass into purpose. The writer of Genesis makes it a six-act story. Each unit in the story has the completeness of a day—a day in the Hebrew style that runs "morning and evening," first day, second day, through the six days, until at last there can be a day of celebration, the seventh day of rest, the Sabbath. The creation unfolds with a kind of simple, dramatic, how-could-it-be-otherwise logic; each element builds on the previous ones in orderly fashion.

But in every symphony (and this creation story surely is a symphony, quite begging for an orchestra and instrumentation capable of supporting it) there ought to be a recurring motif. This symphony has one. In verses 4, 10, 12, 18, 21, and 25 we're told that God saw that what had been done "was *good.*" It's as if the strings said it, then the woodwinds and after that the brass, with each movement having a distinction and a wonder of its own.

There's something almost playful about the story. The God of the universe, the only One capable of envisioning, developing, and bringing to pass such an achievement of creation, seems to take delight in it. This God looks surprisingly like a dedicated craftsman who won't leave the day's work without pausing to see if the work has come out as planned. This God wipes sweat from the divine brow, tucks some eternal measuring instrument into the bib of a holy garment, contemplates the just-completed unit of work, then smiles and says, "*I like it.* This is *good.*"

When this scene repeats itself day after day, one begins to ask questions. Why is this Creator, this ultimate Crafter, so intent upon excellence? Why, after each finished unit, is there this pause, then this almost childlike pleasure in the achievement? Is this Creator so ego-driven as to need repeated reassurance that the work is up to a self-imposed standard? I suppose it's conceivable, if we're judging by human models. Most writers, composers, and artists insist that they are their own most demanding critics, and that they aren't so much concerned with what the public thinks or what the critics say as they are with their own expectation of excellence. They have to know that what they've done is worthy of their own ultimate measure. Those of us who write a book or compose a song like to feel that this passion for excellence is something invested in us by God and that our definition of creativity has some source in the eternal.

Well, it's all right for us humans to live by such a self-measurement. In fact, this attitude is rather admirable when found in us. It means that we look for more from our work than the approval of an audience. We have a dream, and regardless of what others think, we have to live up to our dream.

But we expect more from God. By definition, God doesn't need any self-approval. God knows what God can do. So why does God come to the conclusion of each day's work looking for a favorable evaluation? What compels the Perfect One to evaluate the work of Perfection?

I find the answer near the end of the sixth day of creation. God has now finished man and woman, persons made in the divine image. They are assigned to "have dominion over the fish of the sea, and over the birds of the air, and over the cattle, and over all the wild animals of the earth, and over every creeping thing that creeps upon the earth" (Gen. 1:26). Further, they are told how they are to handle the seeds of the earth and how they are to feed themselves. It's clear that these humans are the climax of the creation process; whatever goes on after this will simply be more of the same. It seems clear that the whole story has been leading to this moment. And the writer of Genesis removes all doubt when he returns to his motif line, because this time the motif comes with full orchestration, all instruments at fortissimo: "God saw everything that he had made, and indeed, it was very good" (Gen. 1:31). Or as the Everett Fox translation puts it, "Now God saw all that he had made, / and here: it was exceedingly good!"[2]

I conclude that this is the moment for which the Creator has been waiting. The whole wonderful process has been building to this moment when the man and the woman are set down in the midst of awesome abundance. Here is the ultimate doting Parent! The infant wears a necklace featuring the Callinan I diamond. The toddler has been given the keys to a Rolls Royce. The prospects are incomprehensible. Only God knows what minerals are in the bowels of the earth, or the uses to which they can be put. And who can guess what resources await on other heavenly bodies—or for that matter, what vitamins and proteins are awaiting discovery in the plants of the earth, what healing properties in some unlikely cactus, or what music in some combination of sounds?

We now know enough about some of the species of our planet that we can calculate how many thousands we make extinct each year. But in truth, we have no way to estimate how many other species are yet undiscovered, or how many are at this moment developing. Sometimes we pause on a clear night and marvel at what is so often open to our viewing. Some of us are grateful at such a moment for the ancient poet who gave us words for such a moment:

When I look at your heavens,
   the work of your fingers,
the moon and the stars that
   you have established;
what are human beings that you
   are mindful of them,
mortals that you care for them?
                    (Psalm 8:3–4)

And at our best we vow to take care of this planet and of any other resources that eventually come to our trust. But we haven't yet found a way of taking inventory on all of this trust. We haven't the remotest idea of our wealth.

Now those of you who are more rational will tell me that I'm carried away. At the least I may seem to have made some leap of logic in moving from the "this is good" of the first five days to the reason for God saying, "this is exceedingly good" on the sixth day. Or you may accuse me of being audacious in the extreme in my claims for our human race. You're amused by what I'm saying because you sense that what I'm demonstrating is not so much the pride that destroys as the pride that is absurd. How dare anyone suggest that God made all this magnificence for the pleasure of the human creature?

Well, in truth the Scriptures say as much, both directly and by inference. And a certain kind of logic reinforces the claim, no matter how absurd the claim may seem to be. After all, who or what else in all of this remarkable creation seems capable of appreciating it? Who else is driven to put their feelings about this creation into poetry or drama, sculpting or painting? Who else or what else in this creation seeks to estimate its wonders, then finally is forced to confess that the best we paint or sing or speak to describe these wonders is inadequate? Not the finest member of the anthropoid family or the most loyal and sensitive canine or the most remarkable porpoise. We alone stand in awe of our universe. We like to say that the birds sing from their love of the Creator; and the prophet Isaiah envisioned a day when "the mountains and the hills . . . shall burst into song, / and all the trees of the field / shall clap their hands" (Isa. 55:12), but we know the prophet is projecting upon nature the impulse we humans have. That is, he is anticipating a day when the rest of creation can respond to its own wonders in the way we humans already, at our best, choose to do. We have this singular gift for standing at wonder of God's creation.

On the other hand, God forgive us, who or what else on our planet can so thoroughly mess up the wonders that surround us? Who else can rape and ravage creation the way we do? Nature may be red in tooth and claw, but it never fouls its own nest as insistently as we do, nor does it seem to have our inclination to destroy its own being. We humans may not grasp the full potential of our planet and the trust placed in us, but we grasp enough to misuse it. If God hasn't developed this "exceedingly good" place for our benefit, we're certainly proceeding as if we held some fee-simple title that allows us to use the property as if it were singularly ours.

But at our human best we marvel at what we have received. In the classic rabbinical view, our "world is good, since goodness is its final aim."[3] It is good not simply in its beauty and its symmetry, but in its source and its purpose. Our world comes from God and is ultimately to achieve the goodness that is inherent in God. And the writer of Genesis says that this earth has been entrusted to us humans—not only its original splendor but also its ultimate fulfillment.

Who deserves such a masterpiece as this, and to whom can its wonders and its frightening potential be trusted? Shall we leave it in the hands and the imaginations of this uncertain biped, this creature that goes so quickly from grandeur to shame, from dancing to depression? This creature, male and female, who will sometimes say of other members of his kind that they're "acting like an animal," not pausing to confess that animals, knowing nothing of free will, would never be capable of such base conduct.

So the wonder of the creation has been trusted to us. God completes the creation, compares it with the divine specifications, and declares it to be "exceedingly good," then puts humans in charge. Yes, and more. God grants to us humans the privilege of enjoying all that has been made; indeed, seems to have invested all this beauty and wonder (most of it yet undiscovered) for our pleasure. God may silence Job by asking him, "Where were you . . . when the morning stars sang together / and all the heavenly beings shouted for joy?" (Job 38:4, 7). But God honors Job by asking him the question. We may not be very articulate in our answer, but we're the only creature to whom God addresses the question.

Now there may be several words to describe what God has done with this creation as outlined in the first chapter of Genesis, but I know of none that says it better than *grace*. This creation is, for sure, *unmerited favor*.

Soon after we finish the first chapter of Genesis we learn that we humans have not done well by this initial gift of grace. We've hurt it so badly, in fact, that the apostle Paul says the creation waits to "be set free from its bondage to decay," and that it is "groaning in labor pains" in anticipation of that day (Rom. 8:21, 22). But what we humans have done to this creation doesn't diminish the grace that first inspired God to make it or to trust it to our care. If anything, our fumblings only underscore the wonder of the grace.

Someone recalls an evening a generation or two ago at a summer resort—the kind that maintained a row of rocking chairs across the grand front porch of the hotel. The vacationers watched the sunset—especially a somewhat overweight, unromantic-looking man who never moved his eyes from the scene. Another vacationer noticed his intentness. "You certainly enjoyed that sunset. Are you an artist?" "No, madam," the man replied. "I'm a plumber, but for five years I was blind."

I struggle often with the worst failure of vision, my dullness in realizing the wonder of the creation that surrounds me. I'm grateful, mind you, but generally in a preoccupied and imperceptive way. Only occasionally do I recognize that the creation is a gift of grace. I haven't earned any of it, from the inchworm working its careful way across the deck of our home to the sun that gladdened this winter day. All of it is unmerited.

But when I ponder the gift, I realize I must care for what is here and I must seek to restore what my ancestors and I have messed up. Because while grace is a gift, those who receive it are obligated to cooperate with its mood. Eleanor Farjeon, who blessed several generations of English children with her stories and poems, saw each morning as part of the same light that "Eden saw play." And seeing it so, she called herself and all of us to "praise every morning, / God's re-creation of the new day."[4]

Call that day—the Eden day or this morning—grace. Grace in the morning.

Chapter 2

God, the Gracious Tailor

Scripture Reading: Genesis 3:1–7, 21

I make no apology for what I said in our opening chapter. Whatever the subject, one has to start somewhere, and what better place to start than at the beginning? I wanted us to know that grace is at least as old as our creation, and to realize that grace may have expressed itself in places where we did not expect it, and in circumstances where we might not have recognized it.

But if there were no more to be said about grace than is revealed in the wonders of creation, grace would be pretty much a one-dimensional affair. It would still be lovely, mind you, but other words might be adequate to describe it—words like generous, beneficent, and wondrous. These are impressive words; I gladly employ them in my worship of God. But fine as they are, they are not in the same category as grace. Of course, I speak with human prejudice. It is at the level of grace that we humans know God most intimately. Words like generous, beneficent, and wondrous describe something of the beauty of God, but not at the point where we need most to know God. Grace reveals God to us at the level of our most poignant need.

Which is to say, grace is most sharply defined when sin is the issue. We speak of grace, you know, as "unmerited favor." It can fairly be said that all the bounties of creation and all the wonders of our human person are unmerited, but in nothing is the unmerited quality demonstrated so forcefully as in God's response to us when we sin. It is quite one thing for you to show kindness to me when I am neutral or perhaps even somewhat likable; it's quite another when in my deeds and

7

attitude I have violated you. So it is that grace takes on its unique character when God encounters us in our sin.

Most of us know the Genesis story to some degree, but bear with me while I review it, because we need its full context in order to appreciate what I want to say. As the writer of Genesis tells the story, God created a universe wonderful beyond comprehension and description. Our generation is particularly equipped to ponder this wonder, because we have gone further in exploring the wonders of this creation than a composite of all the generations that have preceded us. Our exploration has ranged, on the one hand, from walking on the moon and doing a photo-op of Mars, to studying creatures so minuscule that they can build a village on an eyelash. But as awesome as our explorations have been, we now know beyond a doubt that we have touched only the barest shore of an inestimable continent.

I suggested in our opening chapter that God's peculiar pleasure in this creation centered on the human creature. So of course we humans are ecstatically grateful, aren't we? We imagine the man and the woman walking about their domain (and it is their domain; they're to rule over it, they've been told), composing daily songs of gratitude. Well, perhaps they did for a while. I'd like to think that this is the kind of stock from which you and I come. But some time relatively early in their story, they are seduced by the suggestion that God isn't really as beneficent as might appear. The one thing God refuses to Adam and Eve suddenly seems to them to negate all the other good things that surround them. So, ignoring the extravagant kindnesses of a God they know (or ought to know), they buy in with a stranger who raises questions about God's character. And so it has been ever since.

It appears that nothing happened with Eve's action, but when Adam followed suit, "the eyes of both were opened, and they knew that they were naked" (Gen. 3:7). The forbidden tree was the knowledge of good and evil. With their eating, they became conscious of their nakedness. In the simplest terms, they lost their innocence. There has always been an inclination to interpret this event in sexual terms, based on the theme of nakedness. But of course the innocence lost was vastly larger than our sense of sexual identity, just as we are much more than simply sexual creatures.

The point at which sexuality is uniquely significant in this story is in its power to convey life. Of all the power we possess on this earth, none is more closely related to the Creator than the power to pass life on to another generation, or—on the negative side—to take life from another. It was this sense of the sacredness of life that made blood such a crucial symbol to the Jewish people, since "the life of the flesh is in the blood" (Lev. 17:11). Though certainly there is nothing in the Scriptures that would minimize the pleasure of sexual union (indeed, in the Song of Solomon those pleasures are praised), the issue of sexual union is its power to transmit life. Here is the guarantee that life will go on from generation to generation.

I submit that Adam and Eve's new sense of nakedness was not so much an embarrassment at being seen by the other as it was the uneasiness at seeing themselves. Adam wants to hide from Adam. There is nothing I want to hide from another except to the degree that I wish I could hide it from myself. So, too, some issues of which we boast to a particular circle of associates may just as certainly be issues for which we feel extreme embarrassment around those persons who, one way or another, call us to a higher standard. In the presence of such persons, our expectations for ourselves are raised so that we judge ourselves more severely and, in turn, cover ourselves more nervously.

With the loss of innocence there is also deterioration in communication. Children charm us because they are unguarded in what they say. As they lose their innocence, they learn how to say what is expected of them rather than offering their truest feelings. Later in life we realize the importance of true communication, and we seek ways to become open with one another. We long for transparency in others, even as we avoid it in ourselves. We praise vulnerability while we avoid it. We hope to find a friend of such closeness that we will have true communication, but inevitably one or the other of us backs away. We have lost our innocence, and with that loss we have sacrificed the ultimate reaches of communication. Our modern and postmodern culture seems to make clear that it is easier to be physically revealing than spiritually, emotionally, or intellectually revealing. We're afraid of becoming naked.

Adam and Eve are ingenious. Since the era of innocence has ended, they seek a covering. They apprehend the closest thing at hand, the fig leaf. Perhaps the plant's deeply lobed leaves held more promise than other plants. So "they sewed fig leaves together and made loin-cloths for themselves" (Gen. 3:7).

It was a good idea, but an inept one. The fig leaf will too quickly dry up and fall apart at the points of sewing. Like so many of our efforts, the fig leaves are a quick fix and an insubstantial one. A seri-ous theologian might see the fig leaves as an example of salvation by human works. In the broadest sense, this could be so. But I doubt that this is Adam and Eve's first thought. They are not so much seeking salvation as avoiding immediate distress and discomfort. Again, this is consistent with who we are. It takes a while for us to see the more profound, long-range consequences of our deeds. Most of the time I do not so much fear the eternal penalty for my sins as I fear being caught. Hell is not so early in my thoughts as the opinion of my neigh-bors; damnation is not so near as a day in court or a break in health. I'm not sure how sensitive Adam and Eve were to the enormity of what they had done. I'm inclined to think they were more like me; this is why their story makes so much sense to you and me.

When I see the ineptness of the fig leaves, I recognize myself and the humans I have been observing through my lifetime—and through literature, too, for that matter. Francis Thompson confessed that he had fled God not only in the "labyrinthine ways" of his mind, but also through tears, laughter, hopes, and glooms. The variety and contrast of Thompson's list impresses me. As surely as some have made fig leaves of hard rock, others have employed the symphony; for the obvious number who may use alcohol and drugs for a loincloth, there may be a surprising number who use community involvement—which is to say, we shouldn't assume that the fig leaf is an ugly thing. I suspect we like it even better when our fig leaf is aesthetically or philosophically appealing. But it's still a fig leaf if it prevents our fac-ing up to our own souls and to our God.

And this, of course, is our greatest problem. Even when we avoid naming our sins or however able we become in finding synonyms less abhorrent, deep within us we know better, or fear better. And because of that fear, we cannot imagine that God has any sympathy for our predicament. If we felt God could "understand," we wouldn't turn to fig leaves. Being disgusted with ourselves, we conclude that God must be disgusted with us, too. This is part of what makes grace amazing.

Once we get around our own defensiveness we are surprised to learn that God's estimate of us is eternally better than our self-estimate.

The writer of Genesis tells us that God doesn't consider Adam and Eve a lost cause. They have violated God's trust, and have chosen to believe a near stranger rather than a generous God. Instead of turning to God for help, they have hidden; and rather than seeking a divine remedy for their predicament, they have devised makeshift loincloths. So how will God respond?

With *grace*. Quite simply, with grace. "And the LORD God made garments of skins for the man and for his wife, and clothed them" (Gen. 3:21). The fig leaves are patently insufficient. They aren't adequate for the coldness that has now come into human existence, nor will they survive the daily ravages of living. Something substantial is needed. God provides "garments of skins."

Some theologians have seen these skins as expressions of a doctrine of atonement. The skins infer the death of an animal and the shedding of blood, and in this some see a symbol of our Lord's death at Calvary, through which we receive the ultimate covering for our sins. Ephrem the Syrian, the fourth-century theologian, speculated that the skins given to Adam and Eve were created by God at the time for that purpose; but on the other hand he suggested that if animals were in fact killed to provide the skins, the event might have given Adam and Eve a picture of the eventual death of their own bodies.

Whatever extended symbolisms might be seen, the comprehensive picture is grace. The poet in our souls imagines God the Tailor, patiently knitting garments for a wayward creation. Doing so, did God mutter, "Poor fools! Poor, self-destructive fools!" Or did an omniscient God say, "I knew this would happen"? Or did the God who would say a little further along in the human story, "I am sorry that I have made them" (Gen. 6:7) begin already to have such feelings? Were these garments a wondrously Trinitarian achievement, uniting the majesty of the Father, the love of the Son, and the gracious provision of the Holy Spirit in the shaping of the garments? A sentimentalist will picture God weeping as the garments are made, while a pragmatist will see the work being done with holy resignation.

But in every picture, the dominant element is grace. The man and the woman have alienated themselves from God, but God refuses to be alienated. It's very difficult to end a relationship with someone who will not let the hurt be terminal. The man and the woman have gotten themselves in such trouble that their attempt at remedy—fig leaves—is absurdly inadequate; an old phrase says, "They've made their bed, now let them lie in it." God, instead, provides a loincloth.

What was this loincloth? It was an answer to Adam and Eve's predicament. They had brought shame on themselves, and shame is one of the most miserable of companions. They needed to be delivered from the constant reminder of their transgression. Hester Prynne, in Hawthorne's *Scarlet Letter*, is forced to wear a scarlet "A" so that neither she nor anyone in the community will ever forget the wrong she has done. God, in Eden, covers the scarlet letter. And God covers it with a garment of such permanence that it need never again be an issue, unless Adam and Eve allow it to be.

I suspect that even those of us who claim to have accepted Christ's salvation need at times to be reminded of the grace of God the Tailor. We tend to pick away at the scab of shame until we have again inflamed the sore of our shame. Sometimes it is because we refuse to accept the breadth of God's forgiveness. Frederick W. Faber, a Protestant who did all his hymn writing after he became a Catholic priest, warned that we sometimes make God's love "too narrow / By false limits of our own; / And we magnify his strictness / With a zeal he will not own." Grace is sometimes more violated by scrupulous saints than by willful sinners. Grace cannot be effective except as we have the humility to receive it.

And this leads us to the dark side of grace. Dietrich Bonhoeffer warned his generation about the dangers of "cheap grace." I venture we need his message more today than when he spoke it, but of course each generation has had its own inclination toward a sentimental picture of grace. But broad, deep, and wonderful as grace is, there is a toughness to it. That fact is acknowledged in what may well be the most popular hymn in the Western world, "Amazing Grace." Perhaps it is the melody or perhaps the bagpipes that are often used in the musical presentation, but I'm really quite sure most people slip over the unpleasantness of the second line. This grace is amazing, John Newton avers, because it "saved a wretch like me." The venue of grace is the place of our human confession of unworthiness.

So if we are fully to understand the Gracious Tailor, we must meet the Righteous Judge. God confronts Adam and Eve in the Garden. It is a gracious confrontation, since it begins with God's soliciting, "Where are you?" But then God elicits the confession of guilt, after which the multiple sentence is pronounced. And it is only after the man and the woman have been told the price of their disobedience that God prepares the garments that will clothe them. Grace cannot happen without the recognition of wrongdoing. It is not dispensed in a liturgical vacuum.

In truth, Adam and Eve's confessions of sin are rather hazy. In each case, they seek to shunt the blame to another—Adam to Eve, and Eve to the serpent. As Genesis tells the story, God doesn't press them for a more explicit confession; instead, judgment is simply and sharply announced. Their guilt is clear.

And then, the Gracious Tailor makes a garment for each of them, and clothes them. The shame that has come from their bad choice is covered. If their nakedness ever again oppresses them, it will not be the fault of the Tailor.

Chapter 3

The Man Who Refused Grace

Scripture Lesson: Genesis 4:1–16

*G*race is at its unfathomable best when the One who should be sought chooses instead to become the Seeker. This is the principle behind every rescue mission. It is the rationale of every Billy Graham altar call. The God who has been offended seeks out the offender to ask, "Could we somehow make this right?" When John Newton speaks of "amazing grace," it is this very quality that enchants him: "I once was lost, but now I'm found." Newton is not reporting that when he was lost, he found the way home but that when he was lost, someone found him. The finding was not his achievement.

Everyone who testifies to this experience finds it amazing. This is grace indeed, that God would pursue a human creature, not to collect the deserved pound of flesh but to ask the fugitive if he or she would please come home. Those who come home marvel at this divine characteristic. I find something else still more surprising. Some who are so pursued reject the divine suppliant.

There was this man named Cain. He had a very great deal going for him. When he was born it appears that his mother, Eve, thought he was the fulfillment of God's promise. After Adam and Eve's sin, God had said that someday the offspring of the woman would strike the serpent's head. When Eve's first child was born, she seemed to feel that this boy was the one who would make it happen, so she named him *Cain*, which means, "I have gotten."[1] Nearly every mother feels that her child is special, particularly the firstborn, but Eve had extraordinary reasons for thinking this child was special. In time she and Adam had another son, Abel, but apparently with no peculiar sense of his importance.

15

I suppose the boys grew up with normal sibling rivalries. Cain was older, stronger, favored. Nevertheless, Abel was a competitor. Where once the parental world had revolved solely around Cain, now there was another planet of reference. The boys grew up to follow vocational choices, Cain as a tiller of the soil and Abel as a keeper of sheep. In time they brought their offerings to God, offerings appropriate to their work and the only offerings available to them; Cain brought "the fruit of the ground," and Abel brought from "the firstlings of his flock." The biblical writer adds a phrase in describing Abel's offering; he brought the "fat portions." I suspect that this indicates that Abel was doing something out of the ordinary by giving God the choicest parts.

But what was most out of the ordinary about Abel's offering, we learn later from a New Testament writer, was the spirit in which Abel brought it. "By *faith*," the book of Hebrews reports, "By faith Abel offered to God a more acceptable sacrifice than Cain's" (Heb. 11:4). Perhaps that's what is meant by "the fat portions"; perhaps that little phrase suggests that Abel was extending himself by his gift, going the extra mile.

We can't know for sure the specific quality of Abel's faith. Whatever it was, it pleased God and both the brothers sensed it. Abel knew he was blessed and was no doubt grateful, while Cain saw himself rejected and was angry. Indeed, the writer of Genesis says that "Cain was very angry, and his countenance fell" (Gen. 4:5).

I have suggested to you that the New Testament writer explains the difference between the brothers in that Abel worshiped with faith while Cain lacked this quality. It seems to me, however, that we get a strong hint as to Cain's character even without the help of the New Testament writer. We see what must have been lacking in Cain's sacrifice when we see how he reacted to God's response. It's quite clear that Cain wasn't making his offering purely as a gift to God. Some other elements were at work. For one, he was competing with his brother. Now, competition has its place in life, but it's not appropriate to the act of worship. Although worship is often a communal enterprise, each soul is singular before God. You and I are never competing for God's attention; God has time enough for us all. Nor are we competing for God's approval; again, God has more than enough for all of us.

As a matter of fact, the purest worship—like the purest gift—has little or nothing to do with the satisfaction of the worshiper or the giver, but with the satisfaction of the recipient. We seem to have a good deal of misunderstanding at this point. So frequently we judge worship by the pleasure or fulfillment it gives us. There could hardly be a more dramatic perversion. Worship is not about me; it's about God. When I become absorbed with how much worship benefits my person, I make myself the object of worship rather than the God I profess to adore. If in my worship of God I happen also to be blessed it is a happy coincidence, and I can indeed see it is a blessing, because it isn't the point of worship and I am fortunate therefore to receive it. But God is the issue of worship, not I or my pleasure.

Like many of us, Cain missed this fact. Therefore when he saw God's favor bestowed on his brother Abel he became angry. *Very* angry. If Cain had been rational—just rational enough to be self-serving!—he would have asked his brother Abel, "What's your secret? You've succeeded with God and I haven't. How do you do it?" But of course anger destroys our ability to be rational. This is one of the sad facts about anger; by its very nature it causes us to turn in upon ourselves so that we become accomplices in our own destruction.

So Cain's countenance fell. He began to pout. Pouting is one of our less attractive human expressions. As practiced by some, it can be flat-out disgusting; on others it is sometimes so absurd as to be amusing. But never is it winsome. One doesn't want to be around someone who is pouting. Thus, if at this point God is going to pay any attention to Cain, I should think it would be to say rather sharply, "Get over it! You're letting your younger brother be a better man than you are."

Instead God responds with what can only be described as an Old Testament equivalent of grace. God pursues the older brother. "The LORD said to Cain, 'Why are you angry, and why has your countenance fallen? If you do well, will you not be accepted? And if you do not do well, sin is lurking at the door; its desire is for you, but you must master it'" (Gen. 4:6–7).

I consider those three sentences among the grandest in the Bible. I am impressed that God is pursuing this man who—at least at this moment—seems hardly worth the bother. This man, Cain, is unhappy with both God and his brother, and his unhappiness with God takes a

virulent turn. He hates his brother, and it is his brother whom eventually he will kill. But his anger is with God. He doesn't like God's
taste in humans. I submit that when Cain kills Abel he does so as an
attempt to get back at God. "If you like Abel so much," he says by his
attack, "see how you like him dead." Yet God is on the trail of this
unhappy man, this man with murder germinating in his heart. I always
marvel at this quality in God that makes him pursue us humans pre-
cisely when we are most difficult to love.

I'm impressed, too, that God treats Cain like a rational creature.
God reasons with him. If you do well, God says, you will be accepted;
if you don't do well, see where the problem lies—sin is lurking at
your door. But you can handle sin. Sin wants you, but you don't have
to give in to it.

Not only are we humans free moral agents, who can choose between
right and wrong, but we're also creatures who can be reasoned with
when we're doing wrong. Our choice of evil is never, on this earth, our
last chance. A door of repentance lies open before us, because we are
reasonable creatures—or reasoning creatures, if you prefer. So it is the
business of the Holy Spirit to "prove the world wrong about sin and
righteousness and judgment" (John 16:8). We must be capable of such
proving, or the Holy Spirit is wasting a good bit of divine time. I feel
much better about myself in particular and about the human race in
general when I think that God considers us reasonable and that the
Holy Trinity involves itself in appealing to our reasonableness. When
I look back on some of my conduct, I see little evidence of this rational quality. But if God sees it in me, there is hope.

So God reasoned with Cain! What an awesome sight, and what an
early glimpse of grace! This man has failed at worship because he has
been more centered on self than on God. He has brought an offering
but it appears his heart is not really in it. When he sees he has failed
his assignment, he doesn't seek counsel from one who had passed but
chooses instead to mope about with a long face. So God, the Eternal
Suppliant, seeks him out. "Let's talk this over. Think about it, Cain.
You're on the verge of trouble, but you're not helpless. You can still
turn your life around."

I don't know how much thought Cain gave to God's offer or to
God's attempt to reason with him. As the writer of Genesis tells the
story, there is no lapse of time between God's sentence of hope and

Cain's act of violence. It's like one of those movies where we proceed without a break from the father on the telephone with his five-year-old who is saying how anxious she is for him to get home from the office to the father's appearance at the apartment of his mistress. Cain's story is like that. God says, "You must master evil," and Cain answers by going to his brother Abel to invite him "out to the field" where he will kill him.

I don't understand Cain in the particulars of this story because (I'm grateful to say) my instincts toward murder are not strong. But change the details of the scene and I am Cain's clone—not often to the degree of committing evil but to the extent of toying with God. Having heard the divine reasoning, I choose sometimes to answer, "But there are other factors here as well, you know. Doesn't it seem I would be justified if . . . ?"

It appears that Cain didn't wait long enough for grace to get his attention. Francis Thompson said that he fled God "down the nights and down the days," but that God's strong Feet "followed, followed after." I don't know how long God's feet followed after Cain; some people say that God follows us all the way to hell. But there's another element in this divine-human story, which is the element of our response. As I understand it, God respects our human freedom too much to impose himself on us. God is remarkable at pursuit but a failure at imposition.

Which is to say: it is one thing to flee from God, as Adam and Eve tried to do when they hid in the trees of the Garden, and as most of us acknowledge we have done by way of a pathetic variety of self-absorptions; but it is quite another thing to *reject* God. Perhaps that fierce posture of rejection is what we mean by "the unpardonable sin."

But we're left with a question. Why did Cain do it? Why did he reject God's solicitous offer? I think it is because Cain never acknowledged the horrendous quality of his deed or of the mood that preceded it. We can never comprehend the wonder of God's grace until we recognize the shame of our failings; I cannot know how good God is until I have a clearer sense of my own shortcomings. A simple hymn begins,

> Marvelous grace of our loving Lord,
> Grace that exceeds our sin and our guilt![2]

We cannot perceive grace until we understand its necessity. In this, perhaps our generation is at a disadvantage. Our ancestors found grace amazing because they were more conscious both of the reality of sin and of its presence in their own lives. But grace is something of a conundrum to a culture that feels our consummate goal is to think well of ourselves, especially since the well-thinking we seek is a quite superficial kind.

No doubt this was Cain's problem. When he heard God's sentence, he declared that it was more than he could bear. "Today you have driven me away from the soil, and I shall be hidden from your face; I shall be a fugitive and a wanderer on the earth, and anyone who meets me may kill me" (Gen. 4:14). I see no remorse in Cain, no grief over the evil he has done to his brother. At first I thought there was at least some concern about being cut off from God, but I find that in Everett Fox's careful translation the line that reads "I shall be hidden from your face" the real quality is "and from your face must I conceal myself."[3] Like any unrepentant sinner, Cain abhors the penalty he faces but feels no distress over the conduct that has brought the penalty to pass.

So Cain rejected the grace of God. God gave him a mark that would keep others from doing to him what he had done to his brother Abel, but the Genesis writer continues, simply, "Then Cain went away from the presence of the LORD" (Genesis 4:16). Apparently he was quite content to absent himself from God as long as his hide was spared.

It's not a pretty story. All sinners are supposed someday to be sorry and every soap opera ought to end (if it ever does) with the villain acknowledging the error of his or her ways. And especially, grace ought to be rewarded by our human embrace. But the Bible is more honest than soap operas so we don't always get the conclusion we want. I repeat what I said earlier, that those three sentences in which God reasons (indeed, pleads) with Cain are among the grandest in the Bible. Which only makes Cain's dull walking-away all the more inconceivable. But he isn't the only one to treat the grace of God so.

That's very sad, isn't it? It seems that even grace has its limits. Specifically, grace can't be grace until it is recognized as grace.

Chapter 4

Grace in a Brother's Face

Scripture Reading: Genesis 33:1–10

For years I've told my students and colleagues that the Old Testament text I like most to preach is the closing portion of Genesis 32, the story of Jacob's wrestling with the angel. It's a magnificent story of struggle and transformation. I have retold it in any number of sermons, tracing its plotline through varieties of metaphor and interpretative patterns. I've seen grace in God's pursuit of Jacob through his several clever deals and his marginal conduct. But only recently I have come to realize that my sermons have stopped too soon. I have neglected to tell the rest of the story—and the rest is in some ways the best.

Jacob is of course one of the most fascinating characters not only in the Bible but in all of literature. He is the first well-drawn entrepreneur. His close ties to his mother and his distance from his father would fascinate a psychiatrist. He is a man of passion, who adored a woman so much that when he worked seven years to get her hand in marriage, the years "seemed to him but a few days because of the love he had for her" (Gen. 29:20). This love carried through to an unbelievably distorted relationship with his children, so that he became father to a classically dysfunctional family.

And then, there is the story of Jacob and his twin brother, Esau. In all the irregular pieces that make up the complex character of Jacob, none is more significant than Esau.

As the writer of Genesis tells the story, their rivalry began even before they were born. Their parents, Isaac and Rebekah, were delayed in having children. When at last Rebekah conceived, her pregnancy became so difficult that she wanted to die. When she inquired of the Lord, the Lord replied, "Two nations are in your womb, / and two peoples born of you shall be divided" (Gen. 25:23). This could explain to Rebekah the struggling within her womb. But there was more to be said: "the one shall be stronger than the other, / the elder shall serve the younger" (Gen. 25:23). As they emerged from the womb, the older certainly appeared to be the stronger, with his hairy body, but the younger, Jacob, showed a different kind of strength, a tenacity that would mark him all his days. He was born "with his hand gripping Esau's heel" (Gen. 25:26).

This birth scenario seems to have been an indicator of the brothers' continuing relationship. Esau was his father's favorite and Jacob his mother's. Esau was robust, a man of the fields and a hunter, while Jacob was introspective, a quiet man who enjoyed retreating to his tent. In another place and time, you would have found Esau lifting a glass at the tavern or exchanging jokes at the bowling alley, while Jacob would have been lost somewhere in the library stacks.

Because of their very different personalities, if they had not been brothers they would simply have gone their separate ways. But as brothers, especially in a remote household, they were compelled to compete. I suspect this competition manifested itself frequently and in a variety of ways. The Bible reports two landmark instances. In the one case, Jacob gets Esau's birthright for nothing more than an evening meal. The exchange was so audacious that Jacob could have been astonished that his brother accepted the offer, except that Jacob no doubt knew his brother's impetuous nature. Esau was a person of strong feelings and of little patience. When he was hungry, little else mattered. "I am about to die; of what use is a birthright to me?" (Gen. 25:32). In the second encounter Jacob, with his mother's help, flat-out deceived his father and stole the senior blessing from his brother. Where in the first instance Jacob only took advantage of his brother's susceptible temperament, in the second he participated in full-scale theft.

This second occasion brought a complete rupture in the brothers' relationship; Esau vowed openly that when his father died, he would kill Jacob. Jacob migrated to "the land of the people of the east," where he went to work for Laban, his maternal uncle. In time he married Laban's two daughters, Leah and Rachel. In time, he also became very well-to-do. His uncle Laban was a very clever man who didn't mind cheating his son-in-law, but in time Jacob demonstrated that he belonged in the big leagues of marginal finance, while Laban was only a rookie. The same success that compelled him to leave his childhood home now forced him, not unwillingly, to move from the area of his father-in-law and his brothers-in-law.

The writer of Genesis tells us that the angels of God now met Jacob. We're not told what happened in the encounter, but only that Jacob said of the place, "This is God's camp," and that he then "sent messengers before him to his brother Esau in the land of Seir" (Gen. 32:1–3). I assume that something about Jacob's experience with the angels convinced him that he should reunite with Esau. Perhaps the vision of "God's camp" assured him that he was now strong enough to meet Esau; that is, that God's blessing would be with him in measure sufficient to the crisis. Jacob's messengers are instructed to indicate some of Jacob's success to Esau, then to say that he wants to see him "in order that I may find favor in your sight" (Gen. 32:5). After more than twenty years, Jacob wants to make things right.

Why, after twenty years? It may have been entirely pragmatic; Jacob wanted to get home again, to see his parents. Or still more pragmatic, he may have wanted to relieve himself of the nagging fear that someday, somehow Esau would get revenge. Or perhaps, more idealistically, Jacob may have wanted to clear his soul of the unceasing burden of guilt. He may have looked back on his first defrauding of his brother as an example of his own cleverness, unethical as it may have been, but nothing could justify the deception he had practiced on both his father and his brother in the second instance. A person with only a modicum of conscience would want someday to make right such a wrong, and we have reason to conclude that Jacob, for all his faults, was above all a spiritual man. This was what made him, in the first place, so desirous of birthright and senior blessing; he believed in values and traditions beyond immediate gratification.

But when Jacob's messengers returned from their visit to Esau, their report was not reassuring. Esau was coming to meet him, "and four hundred men are with him" (Gen. 32:6). Jacob knew what this meant; he "was greatly afraid and distressed" (Gen. 32:7). So that night, after making proper arrangements for the safety of his family and his possessions, Jacob went alone for the quintessential soul-searching. There he wrestled with a stranger "until daybreak." I'm sure I err in referring to Jacob's opponent as a stranger. Whether the wrestler was a unique messenger of God, or Jacob's conscience, or all the sins of Jacob's past, he was not really a stranger—except to the degree that we allow some of these persons to be so shut from our lives that they become unknown to us, or if we insist on making them *persona non grata.* I said earlier that Jacob's strength was tenacity. So it was that he held on that evening, long after he could no longer win, until something about him was profoundly changed.

He was given a new name, Israel, and he received a blessing from his night visitor. Jacob knew that more had happened than he could ever explain in purely rational terms. He put it in the strongest language available to human perception: "I have seen God face to face, and yet my life is preserved" (Gen. 32:30). Jacob used the language that afterward would be associated with Moses. I suspect that Jacob's language was an impossible hyperbole, but we understand him. Any of us who have longed for a nearness to God—or perhaps, on the other hand, have dreaded it—and have had some moment of exquisite divine agony will resort to absurd exaggeration to describe what is beyond description.

But the tomorrow that was just then dawning was another day, and it was the day he would have to confront his brother, the brother he had long ago defrauded and from whom he had fled, and the brother who was now marching toward him with four hundred men. The writer of Genesis gives us no pause. Our Bibles show a chapter division, but there was none in the original manuscript. We go directly from the wrestling that has left Jacob limping to "Now Jacob looked up and saw Esau coming, and four hundred men with him" (Gen. 33:1).

Our conventional faith stories would now portray Jacob as so faith-possessed that he walks fearlessly into the hosts of the presumed enemy. If one has seen God face to face, why should he fear to meet a mere mortal—and one, at that, whom he has bested time and again in earlier days? But our human faith is not often either so logical or so all-conquering. Jacob organized his fortune and his family for survival, much the way a person in the path of a flood might distribute possessions according to what could more readily be lost and what ought most surely to be saved.

Then Jacob himself led the way, because of course he is the point of issue. As he went, he bowed himself to the ground—a gesture not only of utmost respect but also of subjection; and to make the point altogether clear, Jacob bowed seven times—seven, the number of completeness. If you want a message delivered in body language, you have it here. Jacob has announced as graphically as possible that he is in the subservient position. He is acknowledging what nature declared at their birth, that Esau is first. No matter how many times Jacob has won in the past, and no matter how strategic those victories have been, and how humiliating to Esau, Jacob now puts himself in the dust. Jacob, who less than an hour ago kept his wrestler's hold on God, bows now before his brother.

I suspect this is part of the point. Jacob had to do business with God before he was ready to do business with Esau. More particularly, Jacob had to do business with God before he was ready to subject himself to Esau. Jacob had acknowledged to the divine wrestler that his name was Jacob, *Supplanter, Cheat,* and had been given a new name, Israel, *Prince.* In the confidence of that new name Jacob can deal with the brother who has suffered most from Jacob's flaws of character. The limp Jacob had gotten from the previous night's wrestling makes easier his bowing before Esau.

But Jacob receives a surprise. "But Esau ran to meet him, and embraced him, and fell on his neck and kissed him" (Gen. 33:4). In Jesus' story of the prodigal, we read that when the son came home, "while he was still far off, his father saw him and . . . ran and put his arms around him and kissed him" (Luke 15:20). This was an act of grace, and scholars remind us that it was not seemly for a Middle Eastern father to run to a son, particularly a rebellious one. The language in this Genesis story has the same unlikely extravagance.

Everett Fox, the contemporary Hebrew scholar, has translated the Genesis story with a directness that destroys some of the literary beauty but restores the original emphasis. The issue, Professor Fox points out, is in the Hebrew word for *face.* In the evening before Jacob's encounter with the stranger, he contemplates how he will approach Esau, and he reasons (the italics are Fox's):

> For he [Jacob] said to himself:
> I will wipe (the anger from) his *face*
> With the gift that goes ahead of my *face;*
> Afterward, when I see his *face,*
> Perhaps he will lift up my *face!*[1]

But as Jacob leaves the place of wrestling, en route to his meeting with Esau, he names the place of his holy encounter Peniel, Face of God; and the Fox translation continues (again, the italics are his): "for: I have seen God, / *face to face,* / and my life has been preserved."[2]

Now, embraced by his brother, Jacob's experience is made complete. Esau, in the manner of an elder brother, directs the conversation. "Who are these with you?" Jacob introduces his family, in the order of their place in his affections. Then Esau asks, "What do you mean by all this company that I met?" Jacob explains, "To find favor with my Lord." Jacob's gifts seem very trivial now, as do all our shows of goodness when we are in the presence of grace. Esau replies, "I have enough, my brother; keep what you have for yourself." But Jacob insists that his gifts be accepted, with very good reason. Again, I turn to the Fox translation and his italics: "For I have, after all, seen your *face*, as one sees the *face* of God, / and you have been gracious to me."[3]

One might say that Jacob finds grace twice, first in his wrestling with the stranger and then in the meeting with his brother. I choose to see it, however, as a single, continuing experience, and I believe the writer of Genesis means it to be so. The biblical faith recklessly blends the sacred and the secular, the eternal and the transient. It doesn't allow us to be right with God and wrong with our fellow creatures.

Jacob's experience of divine grace could never have been complete if he had continued to be estranged from Esau. Jacob was transformed by seeing the face of God at Peniel, but he was set free when he saw the face of God in the face of his brother. Mind you, Esau was an unlikely place to see the face of God. Esau was a crude man. All that we have known of him prior to this meeting has shown us a person with little interest in the spiritual. A bowl of soup on a hungry night means more than a birthright to him. Yet with it all, Jacob finds the very face of God in his brother. Specifically, he finds the face of grace.

Grace is God's unique gift, an utterly divine initiative. Its ultimate origin is God, because only God is of such quality as to administer it.

Nevertheless, we humans sometimes convey grace. In some instances the new recipient of grace feels compelled to extend grace to another. I have seen occasions when a new convert wanted immediately to make something right with another. Evangelists of another generation had a word for it: *restitution*. Having gotten right with God, the new convert wanted to make right with others, by acts of restitution. Having received grace, they were drawn to extend a form of grace. Restitution is not, of course, the same thing as grace, but it is a verifiable descendant. Jesus recommended such a mood when he said that when one comes to the altar and remembers that a brother or sister has something against them, one should leave the gift at the altar and "first be reconciled to your brother or sister" (Matt. 5:23–24). In the receiving of grace, one needs to seek a gracious spirit toward others.

I have known the grace of God in my life; indeed, I experience it daily. But sometimes grace has been most accessible to me when it has come to me in the face of another. I remember a friend who asked me if a rumor about me were true. When I assured him it was not, he replied, "I thought as much, and I asked only for clarity. But believe me, if it had been true, it would have made no difference. I would have loved you the same." It was a gracious word. Hearing it, I saw the face of God. Just as Jacob saw grace in the face of his brother, Esau.

Chapter 5

Grace in a Harlot's Tent

Scripture Reading: Genesis 38

A generation ago a Methodist bishop who reviewed books for a denominational publication took on a novel that some readers felt a bishop ought not to read. The bishop replied to the effect that since he had grown up reading the Bible, there was nothing in other literature that would shock him. He might well have had in mind the story of Judah and Tamar.

This chapter-long story may be one of the most important incidents in the Old Testament. The plotline of the Hebrew Scriptures would falter without it; and when the time comes for Matthew's Gospel to transition us into the New Testament story, we would be left with a serious gap. But as important as this story is, we preachers don't often deal with it, probably because it requires so much explaining or omitting, and probably because even after our explaining, some still would find the story offensive. I give you this background so that if you want to skip this chapter, you can. But I hope you won't.

The story seems at first to be an intrusion in the quite fascinating account of the young man, Joseph. Chapter 37 ends with the sentence, "Meanwhile the Midianites had sold him [Joseph] in Egypt to Potiphar, one of Pharaoh's officials, the captain of the guard," and the thirty-ninth chapter begins, "Now Joseph was taken down to Egypt, and Potiphar, an officer of Pharaoh, the captain of the guard, an Egyptian, bought him from the Ishmaelites who had brought him down there." So yes, the incident reported in chapter 38 does indeed appear to break the flow of the Joseph story. But be careful when you criticize a storyteller who has been around as long as the writer of

Genesis has. It's just possible he knows more about his plotline than we do.

It's clear the writer intends the story to be just as it is, because he introduces this new incident with the line, "It happened at that time . . ." (Gen. 38:1). This is the writer's way of saying, "This material belongs here whether you think so or not." He then proceeds to tell a story that covers a period of at least twenty years. The lead character is Judah, a person who came to our attention only a paragraph earlier when Joseph's brothers were trying to decide what to do with their brother Joseph now that they had him at their disposition. Their resentment toward Joseph had grown to the point of violent hatred, so their first inclination was to kill him. Reuben, the oldest brother, delayed this action in hope that he might save the boy's life. But while Reuben was gone, a caravan of traders came by. Judah suggested, "What profit is it if we kill our brother and conceal his blood? Come, let us sell him to the Ishmaelites, and not lay our hands on him, for he is our brother, our own flesh" (Gen. 37:26–27).

It's hard to say whether Judah is motivated by economics ("What profit is it . . . ?") or by humane considerations ("for he is our brother, our own flesh"). I think Judah is pretty pragmatic. He sees a way to be rid of the brother they dislike so intensely, but without feeling blood guilt—and all the while making a nice profit. And of course as a slave their brother will get what they feel he deserves, but it won't come directly by their hand. In a nasty sort of way, Judah is really quite a diplomat; he offers his brothers a win-on-all-sides proposition, including a peculiar feeling of beneficence regarding their brother ("Just think what we could have done!").

This is the first time Judah has a speaking part in the Genesis account. Previously he was identified simply as the fourth son born to Jacob. In a world where the primary favors of inheritance went to the firstborn, the first son mattered most, of course, as the heir, and the second had some possibilities as the spare. But the fourth son had no obvious standing. This was Judah. But when Judah's brothers accepted his counsel regarding selling Joseph to the Ishmaelite caravan, Judah became a key figure in the unfolding plot, because the family of Israel would never become a nation without getting down to Egypt and becoming slaves; and they will get to Egypt via this brother Joseph.

With Joseph on his way to Egypt the story swings over to Judah. The story begins routinely enough. Judah marries a Canaanite woman who bears three sons. In time, Judah arranges for the first son, Er, to marry a woman named Tamar. Something about Er evokes the judgment of God, and he dies. By the law of the times, Judah's second son, Onan, must now marry Tamar, with the first son born to this union to be known as Er's son, since he died without issue. Onan didn't like this arrangement and conspired against it, whereupon he too came under the judgment of God.

Tamar now has legal rights to the third son, but Judah now sees his daughter-in-law as very bad news (trouble seems to follow her), so he doesn't want to endanger this last of his heirs. He therefore sends Tamar home to her father—a humiliating act, in the culture of the times—explaining that she should remain a widow there until the third son "grows up."

In time, Judah's wife dies, leaving him a lonely widower. At about the same time, Tamar recognizes that the third son is now old enough to marry but that Judah is doing nothing to bring this union to pass. Here's where the story gets sticky. Tamar has been terribly wronged. Her father-in-law has shamed her by returning her to her father's house, even if only temporarily, and it is now clear that Judah has no intention of fulfilling his obligation by giving her his third son. So, knowing her father-in-law's habits and patterns and realizing that his time of mourning for his wife is past, Tamar "put off her widow's garments, put on a veil, wrapped herself up, and sat down at the entrance to Enaim, which is on the road to Timnah" (Gen. 38:14). With her face covered, in the fashion of the prostitutes of the time, Tamar was unrecognizable to Judah; he solicited her services, not knowing who she was. He promised to send a kid from the flock in payment, but Tamar insisted on a pledge, Judah's signet, cord, and staff. This was a kind of ancient equivalent to holding a person's credit card as security.

When Judah sent payment with a friend, Tamar was gone, and the friend was told that no prostitute had worked that area; after all, Tamar's stand had been very brief. About three months later, Judah learned that his daughter-in-law had "played the whore," and that she was pregnant (Gen. 38:24). With a fine sense of moral judgment, and exercising the rights that were still his as her father-in-law (in spite of the fact that he had neglected those rights and responsibilities when he sent Tamar home to her father), Judah declared that she should pay for her sins by the penalty of death. Tamar sent her pledge items to Judah, with the message that her pregnancy was with the owner of the signet, the cord, and the staff. Judah got a jolt of conscience. "She is more in the right than I, since I did not give her to my son Shelah" (Gen. 38:26). The Genesis writer tells his readers that Judah "did not lie with [Tamar] again" (Gen. 38:26). Twins were born to Tamar and Judah: Perez and Zerah.

So what is the significance of the opening line, "It happened at that time," when the story that follows is one that covers, as we said earlier, at least twenty years? For one thing, the phrase itself, in the Hebrew, is often used as a literary technique for moving from one scene to another. But ancient rabbis, writing in the Midrash, saw more significance than that. Rabbi Samuel ben Nahman, in commenting on the phrase, "It happened at that time," wrote, "The tribal ancestors were engaged in selling Joseph, Jacob was taken up with his sackcloth and fasting, and Judah was busy taking a wife, while the Holy One, blessed be God, was creating the light of the Messiah: thus IT CAME TO PASS AT THAT TIME. . . . Thus, at the same time that Joseph is sold into slavery, the Messiah is figuratively born."[1]

So if the reader worries that since Joseph is being sold into slavery, evil is apparently triumphing over goodness, the writer of Genesis wants us to know that something else is happening behind the scenes; or perhaps, more correctly, that while one strand of the plot is unfolding with the Midianite traders en route to Egypt, another strand is developing back in Canaan. And of all things, it is happening in the temporary dwelling of a temporary harlot.

Several years ago two of my students took a summer assignment in a mission somewhere in a perilous Chicago neighborhood. When they asked a police officer's help in locating the mission, he showed them the way, but commented, "They seem to insist on putting these missions in the worst parts of town." The church could get no better endorsement, nor could it more surely prove that its ministry is in the genealogy of grace. I concede that the story of Judah and Tamar is not tidy. A moviemaker of questionable credentials would love the plot, and only a few details would have to be changed to give it a contemporary setting: a father-in-law who abuses the legal rights of a defenseless daughter-in-law, but a daughter-in-law who is clever enough to seduce her susceptible kin into an incestuous relationship that results in twins!

If that were all there were to the story, it would be fascinating enough in its own right; we could smile over it as an instance of justice triumphing over crude power. But there is far more. Grace is at work. Grace not only saves from sin, but sometimes it demonstrates itself best in circumstances where sin seems to be in control. It is as if there were a certain perverse cleverness in grace, whereby it wins its victory over evil by turning the instruments of evil in upon themselves. At such times hell must mutter, in the style of the villains in the old-time melodramas, "Curses! Foiled again!"

Simone Weil, the extraordinary French mystic, activist, and social philosopher, pondered grace as she experienced it in her own life. "I have the germ of all possible crimes, or nearly all, within me. . . . This natural disposition is dangerous and very painful, but like every variety of natural disposition, it can be put to good purpose if one knows how to make the right use of it with the help of grace."[2] Which is to say, one should not be surprised to find grace at work in a harlot's tent. In those instances where evil seems to cut a disastrous swath through history as a whole or through our own lives in particular, we can remind ourselves that grace succeeds in manifesting itself through the elements of depravity. Ms. Weil recognized her potential for nearly all possible crimes; she saw also that with the help of grace, this potential could be "put to good purpose." Every sinful soul (which means all of us) should take heart in the same knowledge. We shouldn't presume on this grace by reasoning that our sins will result in God's glory, but at times of despair we should encourage our souls to remember that our sins, our crude machinations, and our stupidities are not greater than God's grace. God can do superior work with inferior materials—seems sometimes, in fact, to glory in doing so.

The ancient rabbis who saw the Tamar story as part of the messianic plan knew they had a sequel in the book of Ruth. For all practical purposes, most readers conclude the book of Ruth with the seventeenth verse of the fourth chapter: "The women of the neighborhood gave him [Ruth and Boaz's son] a name, saying, 'A son has been born to Naomi'" (Ruth 4:17). Thus the widow Naomi, who thought the pleasantness of her life had turned to bitterness, sees her story conclude with a new and more promising pleasantness in the birth of her grandson.

But the big news is in the tedious little genealogy that follows: "Now these are the descendants of Perez: Perez became the father of Hezron, Hezron of Ram, Ram of Amminadab, Amminadab of Nahshon, Nahshon of Salmon, Salmon of Boaz, Boaz of Obed, Obed of Jesse, and Jesse of David" (Ruth 4:18–22). This David, of course, is the shepherd boy who becomes Israel's most beloved king. And in time, as Israel's messianic expectations developed, David was seen as the ancestor of the Messiah who was to come.

But that's not all the book of Ruth has to say about Tamar. When the women of Bethlehem rejoice that Naomi's daughter-in-law, Ruth, is about to marry an aged bachelor or widower, Boaz, they offer her what might seem to be a strange blessing: "and through the children that the LORD will give you by this young woman, may your house be like the house of Perez, whom Tamar bore to Judah" (Ruth 4:12). Perez, one of the twins born to Tamar and Judah, is seen as a particular blessing—a blessing so extraordinary that village women feel it is the loveliest word they can speak to their old friend. Somehow the incestuous relationship of Tamar and Judah has become a heritage of beauty. Why? Because eventually from this line comes Israel's beloved King David. As coaches sometimes say after a difficult game, "It wasn't pretty, but we won."

We readers of the New Testament pick up the plot in the Gospel of Matthew, as that writer gives us the genealogy of Jesus, the Messiah. Jacob is "the father of Judah and his brothers, and Judah the father of Perez and Zerah by Tamar" (Matt. 1:2–3). So it is that the messianic line unfolds. It may not seem like a direct route, but life's plots rarely follow the shortest, neatest line between two points.

No wonder, then, that the writer of Genesis interrupts the story of the patriarch, Joseph, to recount a saga of twenty years or more that probably began while Joseph was still a boy at home, and continued when he was in prison or was already the prime minister. But the two strands of the plot have to develop simultaneously: we must get the family of Jacob down to Egypt so they can become a nation rather than losing their identity by intermarriage with the peoples around them, and we must have a line that will produce Israel's great king, David, and eventually the Messiah.

And the interruption will happen in the temporary tent of a temporary harlot. Don't try to fence in grace. To do so would diminish its wonder.

Chapter 6

Grace Once a Week

Scripture Reading: Exodus 20:8–11

*O*nce upon a time there was a nation of slaves. They had been slaves for generations, for so long that no one living could remember a time when they were not slaves; so long, in fact, that no one living could remember even talking to someone in their nation who remembered freedom. In their minds, to associate themselves with freedom seemed mythic, with no connection to real history.

Then they got freedom, under a remarkable leader named Moses, and they set out upon a new life. But old habits and ways of thinking are slow to die. You can take a person out of slavery in one dramatic political act, but to take the slave out of the person may require a lifetime. It may, in fact, never happen, emancipation proclamations notwithstanding. This is especially true in matters having to do with work, because most of us, whether we are slaves or free persons, have to spend a good piece of our time working. And when you're working, you may not clearly distinguish the difference between your role as a free laborer and your role as a slave.

So not long after the slave nation Israel had been set free from slavery and had been delivered from the land of their captivity, Egypt, and while they were still on the way to the land that had been promised to them, God gave them a wonderful gift. Let me call it a gift of grace, a grace to be celebrated once a week. God gave them the *Sabbath*. And because we humans are sometimes peculiarly skeptical about gifts, God made the Sabbath a law. It was part of that remarkable document we call the Ten Commandments.

And here's something interesting. This commandment is by far the longest of the ten. It goes into specific details, as if to make sure there is no misunderstanding and as if to guarantee full compliance. The details may seem tedious to you and me, but obviously they are listed for a purpose, part of which is our protection and blessing:

> "Remember the sabbath day, and keep it holy. Six days you shall labor and do all your work. But the seventh day is a sabbath to the LORD your God; you shall not do any work—you, your son or your daughter, your male or female slave, your livestock, or the alien resident in your towns. For in six days the LORD made heaven and earth, the sea, and all that is in them, but rested the seventh day; therefore the LORD blessed the sabbath day and consecrated it" (Exod. 20:8–11).

For the commandments regarding murder, adultery, theft, and false witness, it's enough simply to say *No*, but in this commandment, specifics are spelled out and a reason is given—a reason with its roots in God, eternity, and creation. It could be argued that this commandment is so specific because its rationale is not as obvious as is the case with murder, adultery, and theft, and certainly this is true. But there's more to it. The word "Remember," for instance, suggests some sort of prior understanding—as indeed there is, because the Sabbath is for the Jewish people a sign of their covenant relationship with God. And consider the quality that is to be brought into this Sabbath observance; it is a day to be kept "holy." That is, this day is to be different than other days; it is a day to be set apart.

And then there is the relationship of this day to the world of work. Six days we labor and do all our work, but the seventh day is in a class by itself, a day set aside to "the LORD your God." Ours is a world of work. Work is necessary to us, for survival, but it is more than just the activity of a grazing creature for whom life is nothing more than simple sustenance. We see work as honorable, demonstrating our worth, and yet by its very nature work can become an evil, an all-consuming creature. So it is that there must be a cessation to it, a time to pause, to reflect, to be set free. And "set free" is the proper term. If we are not set free at regular intervals, we are still slaves. It may be a voluntary slavery, as is the case with the workaholic or the accumulateaholic, but it is still slavery, because it makes a human being one-dimensional. And humans are more than that. Made, as the Bible describes us, in the image of God, we are creatures who inhale and exhale, who ebb and flow, who work and rest.

Herein was the grace of the Sabbath. It came to a slave people, a people who knew they were slaves and had been so designated, and it told them their worth. Benno Jacob, a German rabbi in the first half of the twentieth century, said that the Sabbath "removed with one stroke a contrast between slaves who must labor incessantly and their masters who may celebrate continuously."[1] A people who had bowed daily under enforced labor were now able to walk upright on all days because a day each week was established specifically for their celebration. Hermann Cohen, a German-Jewish philosopher who lived from the middle of the nineteenth century until nearly two decades into the twentieth, said that the Sabbath was "the first step on the road which led to the abrogation of slavery," and that if Judaism had brought nothing else into the world, this would be enough to prove itself a "producer of joy and a promoter of peace" for humankind.

Cohen went on to apply this principle to those free people who are forced to live within the strictures of poverty or of discrimination. "The ghetto Jew discarded all the toil and trouble of his daily life when the Sabbath lamp was lit. All insult and outrage was shaken off. The love of God, which returned to him the Sabbath each seventh day, restored to him also his honor and human dignity even in his lowly hut." As such, Cohen said, the "Sabbath became the most effective patron-saint of the Jewish people."[2]

The Sabbath was a gift. Thomas Cahill points out that "no ancient society before the Jews had a day of rest." He calls it "surely one of the simplest and sanest recommendations any god has ever made."[3] I think it significant that the story of the giving of the Law at Sinai concludes in Exodus with God saying to Moses, "You yourself are to speak to the Israelites: 'You shall keep my sabbaths, for this is a sign between me and you throughout your generations, given in order that you may know that I, the LORD, sanctify you.'" It is to be "a perpetual covenant," "throughout their generations"; "a sign forever between me and the people of Israel that in six days the LORD made heaven and earth, and on the seventh day he rested, and was refreshed"

(Exod. 31:12–13, 17). The grand declaration that began with "I am the LORD your God, who brought you out of the land of Egypt, out of the house of slavery" (Exod. 20:2) concludes, so to speak, with "I am the LORD who gives you rest." The Sabbath is a gift, a gracious gift.

And because the Sabbath was a gracious gift, it was to be extended to others. It would hardly be grace if it were a mean-spirited gift. So Israel was to extend the Sabbath benefits not only to son and daughter, but also to "your male or female slave, your livestock, or the alien resident in your towns" (Exod. 20:10). The Sabbath may be a covenant symbol between God and Israel, but it is too good a thing to confine to Israel; even slaves and alien residents are meant to benefit. It is a singular gift to the Jew, but a favor to all humanity if they will receive it. Yes, and nature, too. Grace, indeed!

Why such beneficence? Because "in six days the LORD made heaven and earth, the sea, and all that is in them, but rested the seventh day; therefore the LORD blessed the sabbath day and consecrated it" (Exod. 20:11). So humanity is to rest, not simply because they have been commanded to do so, but because the very God has done so. We worship a God who works and a God who then rests; now you be like that! What a lovely idea! Both the working and the resting are divinely ordained; each has its place in God's plan. There is not a particular command to work; the necessity of survival is command enough. But survival is such a compelling thing that we might sanctify it beyond its right, so God sets a boundary on work and gives holy honor to rest.

The problem, of course, is to keep the holiness there. Some other generations turned the holiness into legalism so that the celebration became a calendar of restrictions. Our generation is in little danger of such legalism; we have lost the Sabbath in license, turning celebration into frantic activity.

At its worst, Judaism turned the Sabbath into a thicket of legalisms, and it was to these legalisms that Jesus reacted so vigorously. His answer was simple and direct: "The sabbath was made for humankind, and not humankind for the sabbath" (Mark 2:27). In those few words Jesus was essentially paraphrasing the commandment: God gave us the Sabbath so that we might enjoy rest. The regulations were well meaning in that they were intended to implement the Sabbath, but in practice they succeeded rather in changing its very nature. We Christians, particularly at times in the Reformed and Holiness traditions, have been equally zealous in compiling restrictions rather than rejoicing in God's generosity. I suspect there is always a hazard in institutionalizing grace. Unmerited favor isn't consonant with meticulous exclusions.

Some of the loveliest suggestions for Sabbath observance have come to us over several centuries from a variety of rabbis. So a third-century rabbi said, "The Sabbath was given only for pleasure." This is such a beautiful thought, but one that we may not easily grasp—not because we are so legalistic about the Sabbath but because our definition of pleasure is so limited. A culture that equates entertainment with pleasure is hardly prepared for the further reaches of pleasure. "Sanctify the Sabbath with food, drink, clean garments and pleasure," the same third-century rabbi wrote. We understand how food, drink, and clean garments have something to do with pleasure, but we miss the significance of *sanctify*. The Talmud Jerushalmi instructed, "Devote part of the Sabbath to Torah and part to feasting." I submit that this was a call to continual feasting—first of a spiritual and intellectual kind, in the study of the Torah, God's Law, and then of a physical kind.

These teachings, it seems to me, were intended to heighten all the ordinary pleasure of life. Do you enjoy a Sunday afternoon nap? You should; you should enjoy it in a manner unlike any other day. A Jewish scholar three and a half centuries ago said, "Sleep on the Sabbath is a pleasure." God smiles on this Sabbath rest; it reflects the divine pleasure at the completion of creation. Rabbis taught that married couples received additional blessing for sexual union on the Sabbath. "Tell nothing on the Sabbath," the Sefer Hasidim instructed, "which will draw tears." This Hasidim warns at another point that we should not nap on the Sabbath in order to work better the next day, "for Sabbath rest is for Sabbath enjoyment, not for the sake of a weekday's work." That is, the Sabbath is not a utilitarian instrument; it is an end in itself, and its end is rest. And the rest that it offers is more than a good night's sleep, much more than a drug-induced relaxation; it is a time of pure relaxation. The emphasis, let it be said, is on the word *pure*.

All of which is to say, the Sabbath—this once-a-week gift—was to be pure grace. It was not earned by six days of labor, though only those who have labored have a measure by which to appreciate some of its qualities. Nor was it only for God's chosen people, although it was a mark of their covenant; as we noted earlier, Israel was to extend the Sabbath's benefits to the alien in their midst and to the stranger within their gates. The Sabbath was a gift! God had indulged in rest in celebration of the creation and chose now to recommend the same exquisite favor to the human creature and those animals the humans employed.

But something in us humans struggles with grace, whatever its expression, and so it has been with the gift of the Sabbath. In Jesus' day the Jewish religious leaders had reduced the Sabbath to scores of complicated laws. With great scholarship and with quite earnest and self-serving piety, they made the Sabbath into a burden. God had given them the Sabbath to celebrate, and they had reduced it to a religious debate.

We Christians have done no better. Some generations have made the day so strict that the aim seems to have been discomfort. So Jean Rhys, the twentieth-century British novelist, said that the "feeling of Sunday is the same everywhere, heavy, melancholy, standing still."[4] One can't be sure whether Ms. Rhys is complaining of a legalistic Sabbath, or whether it is simply that she has missed the mood of the day's original intent. I remember a society in which so-called "Blue Laws" meant that Sunday baseball games in some cities had to be completed by a certain hour of the afternoon, and where virtually every store was closed. If any law operates today, I suspect it would be a "Bottom Line Law," which argues that without Sunday sales, a business—particularly in a shopping mall—can't show a profit. Someone has said that the Bible invented the weekend. If so, we've done pretty well at ruining the invention.

A grand Jewish tradition contended that if Israel would keep just one Sabbath properly, as intended, the Messiah would come. Why? Because the Sabbath was equivalent to all the commandments. It was a foretaste of the perfect age. It represented a tranquility in which murder, theft, adultery, and coveting seemed quite impossible. It suggested a world in which work is honored not simply by daily sustenance but also by the privilege of absolute escape from work. The story of Israel's manna in the wilderness is instructive; there would be enough manna on the sixth day so that there would be no need to collect on the seventh day. In a very real sense, the Sabbath was a rebuke to worry; there is enough in God's creation that one need not work every day. Here is a lesson that should be learned by any of us who feel so much pressure in our work that we can never be free of it: take a day off! God, with a whole universe to run, rested; we assume our responsibilities greater than God's when we cannot step back one day a week. The Sabbath is an act of faith; there is more to life than work, and God can be trusted to keep our small universe running while we take a day-deep breath.

But such a grasp of the Sabbath depends on our recognizing that God has given us this day for the peculiar holiness of pleasure. It is a day to *enjoy*. But this enjoyment is beyond secular definitions. It is not necessarily pious, but it is godly. It is not painfully religious, but it is full of wonder, of thanksgiving, of gladness, and of grace. Because the truest kind of rest is God's gift, and because the truest kind of joy—the only real joy—is from God.

Chapter 7

Gracious Commandments

Scripture Reading: Deuteronomy 5:1–7

*T*heologians are like politicians, novelists, and pop music stars in that they have their day and then fade into oblivion. I find that some of the theologians I studied in my seminary days are unknown to the students who are now in my classes; when I mention their names, I draw a dull stare. Even more surprising, the most venerable and seminal of all Christian theologians, the apostle Paul, is currently unpopular with some segments of the contemporary theological community. Personally, I like Paul a very great deal; I wish I could have known him. But I'm sorry about one thing. He gave the Old Testament Law a bad name.

I understand why he did it. In truth, it was absolutely necessary that he do so. I think Paul loved the Commandments as fiercely as did any of the prophets of Israel, but he had to make clear the difference between Christianity and Judaism, and to do so he had to explain the peculiar boundaries of the Law. In the process, Paul seemed to discredit the Law, just as one seems often to destroy a particular person or position in the process of showing the unique value of another. During the Reformation, Martin Luther brought still more emphasis to the difference. Law is seen as the essence of the Old Covenant and Grace as the spirit of the New. I'd be among the first to agree that the difference between Law and Grace is profound. But it's a difference within the family. Which is to say, there is something very gracious about the Commandments, the centerpiece of the Hebrew Law.

That's the point Moses made in the presentation of the Commandments, as reported in the book of Deuteronomy. At Mount Sinai,

Moses had served as the negotiating attorney between God and Israel. So when he convened Israel in the setting described in the book of Deuteronomy, in what is pictured as his valedictory to his people, he reminded them how they had first received the Law. He began by admonishing the people: "Hear, O Israel, the statutes and ordinances that I am addressing to you today; you shall learn them and observe them diligently" (Deut. 5:1). Though this document is made up of "statutes and ordinances," Moses refers to it as a *covenant*, an agreement God had made with the people. We want to come back to that detail, because it is near the heart of the matter.

The scene Moses describes is nothing less than epochal. The Lord, he said, had spoken with them "face to face at the mountain, out of the fire" (Deut. 5:4). The experience had been so overwhelming that the people were afraid, so Moses had stood "between the LORD and you." Moses' use of the term "face to face" is especially interesting. At one time in his communion with God, Moses had asked for the privilege of seeing God's face, and had been refused; he was allowed only to see God's back, as the Lord passed by (Exod. 33:12–23). But now, as Moses reviews with the people the events at the giving of the Law, he speaks of it as a "face to face" occasion. I think this is Moses' way of helping the people comprehend the profound wonder of what had happened. How big was this event of the covenant? So big that God made a personal appearance to implement it. This was too big an event to trust to angels or any other intermediaries. For such a covenant as this, God must look the people in the eye; and they, in turn, must look into the face of God as they receive the Law, because the Law was for them—and for all succeeding generations—a view of God. It was more than a document; it was a divine visitation.

Thomas Cahill says that in the Ten Commandments we have the first and probably the last time that "human beings are offered a code without justification. Because this is God's code, no justification is required."[1] There is a decided and dramatic finality about these Commandments; they are presented without justifying argument and usually with few clarifying details: no other gods, no graven images, no murder, no adultery, no stealing. In sum, no equivocating and no exceptions. As we read further in Exodus, Leviticus, and Deuteronomy, we find details of the law spelled out, to assure their being understood, but even then the sense of finality prevails. If any justification is given, it is the straightforward phrase, "I am the LORD your God" (Lev. 19:4, 10, 12, etc.). Does this sound imperious? It's meant to. The Ten Commandments didn't come out of a plebiscite, nor were they a report from a study and research committee. No wonder, then, that Moses speaks of the giving of the Law as a "face to face" visit by God.

But with all of that, the Law was a *covenant*. God was entering into an agreement with a certain segment of the human race, to the eventual benefit of the whole human race. See the divine humility. God chooses to relate to us creatures, fully knowing that relationships so easily become messy. All of us humans have times when we would like to absent ourselves from the rest of the human race, because of the pain that is inevitable in relating to others. From our experience, we might judge that God would be justified in avoiding such disappointment. Instead, God chose to enter a covenant.

And while the details and requirements of the covenant were entirely of God's choosing, the benefits were all Israel's—and eventually, as Israel's younger siblings, all ours. "Do these things, and you shall live." To use an old phrase, as old probably as the first frontier evangelist by the rivers of Babylon, we don't break the Commandments, they break us. If we violate them, they remain, but we are broken. Perhaps this is because, as Cahill as said, "they are written on human hearts and always have been. They were always there in the inner core of the human person—in the deep silence that each of us carries within."[2]

So it is that these Commandments are altogether to our benefit. We want a world where no one kills, where vows of marriage and of daily friendship are never violated, where all doors can be left unlocked, where no one lies to us or about us; indeed, where no one casts aspersions that can be as damaging as lies. We wish for a world where our neighbors rejoice in our good fortune, not envy us and covet what we have. We wish for a world where no one bows down to the images of our own making, the stuff urged upon us daily by the mills of advertising and public relations. We wish, that is, for a world where God is God—and where everyone lives by the Ten Commandments. Such a world sounds so idyllic that we smile and continue cynically and despairingly in the world as it is. We forget that much of the matter is really very simple.

You see my point. The Law is not an evil thing. No wonder a poet of Israel sang, "Oh, how I love your law! / It is my meditation all day long" (Ps. 119:97). Because we humans have always been human, I have no doubt that some ancient Israelites scanned the Law in search of loopholes, much the way an unscrupulous lawyer might do with the legal code. But the ecstasy of the ancient is convincing. When he goes without pause from marveling at the heavens that tell the glory of God and the firmament that proclaims God's handiwork to the same excitement over the wonders of God's Law (Psalm 19), one knows that the devout Jew found loveliness in the Commandments that was the furthest thing from grudging obedience.

But again, the point was the covenant. Above all else, the Bible is a covenant book; thus we refer to its two parts as the Old and New Testaments, or covenants. The concept first appears in the story of Adam and Eve, but it takes on its plotline form in God's call to Abraham and Sarah, when a promise is given for the future benefit of the whole human race. As the covenant develops in Exodus and Deuteronomy, it identifies the divine plan for God's working with a specific nation. This nation is therefore known as a people "holy to the LORD your God." This quality of holiness is not something they have achieved; it is conferred upon them by their being called into the covenant.

Scholars sometimes remind us that the biblical covenant cannot really be compared with the usual contract or agreement, because other agreements are between two equals (though a person seeking a mortgage would question their equality with the bank in such an instance). No matter; the covenant described in Scripture has this quite breathtaking quality. As I suggested earlier, God takes on an unlikely position for the deity, and a humble one, in soliciting the human creature to enter into a contract. Nevertheless, God is God and we are not. So Moses makes clear that this contract contains both curse and blessing. "See, I have set before you today life and prosperity, death and adversity." Obey the Commandments "and the LORD your God will bless you in the land that you are entering to possess." Turn away from these Commandments, and "you shall perish" (Deut. 30:15–18). Now while there is an element of threat in such a covenant, the security remains. Israel could say, as might a professional athlete, "I'm under contract." With the contract comes security. But with it also come restraint and responsibility. Dorothy Sayers, the British novelist and lay theologian, said, "If men will not understand the meaning of judgment, they will never come to understand the meaning of grace."[3] The very severity of the contract gives proportion to the quality of its grace.

Still and all, anyone signing a contract might feel uneasy. Can the initiating party be depended on—especially when that party is in every way so superior? Since this initiating party has so decided an upper hand, are we in danger of the whims and vagaries that are so easily exercised by one in power? Particularly, on what basis does God issue this series of Commandments? This is the crucial element, the character of the initiator. See, then, how right it is that the Commandments begin with an announcement about the character of God. This character is not couched in pretty, descriptive words, but in a deed, and the deed speaks for itself. "I am the LORD your God, who brought you out of the land of Egypt, out of the house of slavery"; and then, the first of the Commandments, "you shall have no other gods before me" (Deut. 5:6–7).

The peoples among whom the Israelites lived worshiped gods associated with nature. Israel saw the wonders of God in nature, but never to the point of confusing God with nature. Nor was it these natural wonders that impressed them most. Thus the covenant does not begin with "I am the LORD God, the maker of heaven and earth," though such power is surely awesome. But God's claim is not based on power, but on character. This is a God who is touched by the state of human infirmity, and who finds it unthinkable that a people should be bound in slavery.

Mind you, this, too, is power. But it is power of a different kind than that which demonstrates itself in the acts of creation. We are speaking here of *moral* power. The people of Israel, recalling their national history, see themselves as beneficiaries of this moral power—a power that exercises itself through the instruments of nature, so that in their crisis hour a "strong east wind" drives back the sea and turns the sea bed "into dry land," so the Israelites can pass through (Exod. 14:21–25). But the wonder of nature is not as impressive as the wonder of God's character, in that God would choose to deliver Israel.

Lord Acton, the insightful nineteenth-century British historian, wrote his contemporary, Bishop Mandell Creighton, "Power tends to corrupt and absolute power corrupts absolutely." The words should be posted in the office of every government administrator, every corporate executive, every line boss, every athletic coach, indeed, every denominational executive and parish pastor or priest. Nothing reveals character as sharply as the way we use power. It is very nearly impossible to exercise power without treading the dangerous edges of corruption, and the more power we have, the greater the danger. Since, by definition, God has absolute power, I want to know the character of the God I worship; and particularly, I want to know the character behind the laws this God enacts. To put the matter in the simplest terms, I want to be sure God can be trusted with all this power. Suppose he can't, someone asks; what will you do about it? Nothing. But I promise that such a god won't get my worship. That independence is my feeble human prerogative. I want a God with admirable character.

This is the point Moses makes as he reminds Israel of the covenant that binds them to God, and the particulars of that covenant that we know as the Law. This Law tells them of the character of God, and that it is character they can depend upon. Israel knew something about the gods of their neighboring nations; petulant gods that destroyed at any whim, gods that called for the burning of sons and daughters, gods carved from a tree stump, and gods whose moral conduct would shame even the shoddiest of humans. Moses wanted Israel to understand how different was the Lord God, the one who had called them out of Egypt's bondage. This was a God who opened the Red Sea to make a passage for the people, and who led them through the forty years of their wilderness rebelling.

So it is that the issue is summed up in the opening Commandment. "I am the LORD your God, who brought you out of the land of Egypt, out of the house of slavery; you shall have no other gods before me" (Deut. 5:6–7). All else follows from this. If God is God alone, then there is no question of the right to lay out the Commandments that follow. These Commandments are simple and basic. They are, to use a contemporary term, "user friendly." Obey them and life goes well; disobey them and life becomes complicated at best and destructive at worst. They provide us with boundaries, to protect us from life's hazards. "This is the way," they say; "walk ye in it."

And it is *good*. The apostle Paul will remind us later that it is not a saving way, but it is a good way. It is also an essential way, because as Paul—again—explains, we wouldn't know sin if it weren't for the law and the definitions the law provides. So the law informs the conscience, and provides a setting in which conviction can work, to the eventual correcting of our transgressions.

And when obeyed, these laws are *very* good. They help us live better, and they make us better to live with. Having found salvation in Christ, the truest Christian becomes the best advertisement for the law. Such a Christian sings harmony to the ancient Hebrew poet's melody:

> The law of your mouth is better to me
> than thousands of gold and silver pieces.
> (Ps. 119:72)

Whatever else we say of the law, remember that it is *gracious*. It is God's good gift.

Chapter 8

God's Unlikely Choices

Scripture Lesson: Deuteronomy 7:1–8

*I*t is William Norman Ewer who said it most memorably and succinctly:

> How odd
> Of God
> To choose
> The Jews.

Ewer was an able but relatively unknown British writer, but those
eight words in four lines have won him a place in books of quotations;
as far as I can find, his only place. I don't know whether Ewer spoke
from reverence or from prejudice, but thousands of persons before
and since have pondered the same question, even if not phrasing it so
memorably. Those who have raised the question have done so with
motives and emotions ranging from the most noble to the most con-
temptible. But the mystery remains: Why did God choose the Jews?

If someone reading this chapter hasn't heard of God's choice, let me
hasten to say that it is one of the basic declarations of the document
Christians call the Old Testament and that Jews call simply the Scriptures. And if you're disposed to discard some teachings of the Old Testament in favor of what appears in the New, let me add that the New
Testament affirms the theme, especially in the Epistle to the Hebrews
and in Paul's Letter to the Romans. People argue about almost every
subject in the Bible, but hardly anyone will deny that the Bible declares
the peculiar role of the Jews as chosen. Some resent it, including some
who should know better; some question God's wisdom in the choice

(though not necessarily putting it that way, lest they be guilty of irreverence); and some thank God that it is so. But it is difficult to deny that this is the Bible's position, in both the Old and New Testaments.

If it will make some feel any better, the Bible itself acknowledges that the Jews were an unlikely choice. And it does so, not in some obscure passage, but in the book of Deuteronomy, in that section of the Scriptures held most sacred among the Jews, the Torah. Moses, the deliverer of Israel and the premier lawgiver, makes the declaration in what is presented as his final address to the people he has led from slavery up to the border of their land of promise. In the fortieth year of their erratic journey from Egypt to Canaan, "on the first day of the eleventh month, Moses spoke to the Israelites just as the LORD had commanded him to speak to them" (Deut. 1:3), reciting their divine history and reviewing the Law, their sacred covenant with God. Then, in chapter seven, he explains why God has chosen them.

Like any good preacher, novelist, or playwright, Moses lays a foundation of suspense. He explains that when Israel arrives at the land which they will soon "enter and occupy," they will find that other nations are already there. Moses lists them: Hittites, Girgashites, Amorites, Canaanites, Perizzites, Hivites, and Jebusites. Moses adds: "seven nations mightier and more numerous than you" (Deut. 7:1). It is not by chance that seven nations are involved. Seven is the number of completeness in the Bible, so the inference here is that these nations represent a kind of symbolic totality. Other nations exist, of course, but these seven become representative of the opposition Israel was to face; indeed, perhaps representative of the opposition they have dealt with through all the centuries of their often-troubled history.

Moses wants particularly to remind his people that these nations are "mightier and more numerous" than the Jews. He is building a case. He wants his listeners (and eventually, his readers) to raise the question, "Why the Jews?" He is preparing us already for the fact that the choice is unlikely. Is God looking for a mighty people? If so, there are at least seven in the immediate territory who are mightier. Might God be interested in a "numerous" people? Again, if so, there are at least seven who qualify, and God won't have to go far to find them.

We modern readers realize that these seven peoples are essentially unknown to us today. The spell-checker on my computer acknowledges only three of them: the Hittites, the Amorites, and the Canaanites; the others are simply errors in the computer's system. But the truth is, these nations were powerful and successful in their time. The Canaanites were an advanced civilization, with laws and customs that influenced other peoples until at last the Canaanites lost their identity to the Phoenicians. The Hittites were a dominant political and military power in the Middle East for nearly seven hundred years. Their system of writing, hieroglyphics, contributed to the continuing culture of the Middle East. When Moses speaks of these nations as mighty and numerous, he has some data on his side. But the fact remains that none of us today has any Hittite, Girgashite, or Perizzite friends, while a great many of us count Jews in our circle of friends and associates, and all of us take for granted that the Jews as a people and Israel as a nation will be part of the world news on any given day.

Moses' instructions to the Jews regarding their relationship with these nations are severe to the point of inhumanity. In truth, Israel didn't succeed in fulfilling Moses' instructions. Israel was to wipe out the civilization of these nations, particularly at the point of their religious practices. There was a reason: "For you are a people holy to the LORD your God; the LORD your God has chosen you out of all the peoples on earth to be his people, his treasured possession" (Deut. 7:6).

"Holy" is a key word. We think of "holy" as a position or person ethically or morally superior, which is surely an admirable goal. But basically, "holy" means a person or an object that is set apart for divine purposes. The objects Israel used in its temple were basically common, even if beautifully crafted of expensive materials; a basin is still a basin, a lamp stand a lamp stand. But they became holy because of where they were located and the purpose for which they were used. The priests were to be dedicated with "a holy anointing oil." A warning came with the instructions: "It shall not be used in any ordinary anointing of the body, and you shall make no other like it in composition; it is holy, and it shall be holy to you. Whoever compounds any like it or whoever puts any of it on an unqualified person shall be cut off from the people" (Exod. 30:32–33). No one was likely to bottle the compound with a label, "Made by the Perfumer to the Levitical Priesthood." The item was set apart, holy; it was to be used for no other purpose.

And so with Israel. They were to be holy. At best this implied ethical conduct altogether unlike that of the nations around them. But substantively, it meant that they were to be a *different* people, dedicated to God's purpose and used as God might desire and command. On the surface, their events might not have seemed that different from those of the neighboring nations. As their history unfolded, they, too, had kings. They, too, engaged in wars. But Israel's kings were judged, not by the buildings erected during their reign or by their victories over their enemies, but by their faithfulness to the Lord God. As each king is evaluated in the books of Kings and Chronicles, the judgment is always at this issue: were they true to the Lord their God? And the standard of measure in most instances was King David, a person after God's own heart—not a perfect man, but one who desired to do God's will and who repented when he did not.

When we speak therefore of Israel being God's "chosen people" we should remember that it's not in the sense of their being God's favorites—not, at least, in the sense of entitlement. Rather, they were chosen the way a coach might choose a quarterback. Or many a Jew, looking back on the history of his people, might say, as a general choosing an elite unit to go into a battle where the chances of survival are small. But believe me, while such an assignment may be frightening in the extreme, it is still a huge compliment. If the general judges that I'm the one best able to bring off the nearly impossible, the peril itself becomes a tribute.

But still and all, why Israel? Why the Jews? In truth, this is a question whenever one considers the matter of a holy calling. I teach in a theological seminary where the majority of my students—perhaps all of them—feel they are called of God. Some have left profitable professions in law, business, engineering, teaching, or computer science to begin at the bottom in Christian ministry. Many uproot their families to reinvent their lives at the bridge of their thirties and forties. Men and women believe so earnestly in their spouse's call that they leave their work to accompany their companion to seminary, laboring to see them through to a place of ministry.

As I look out on such classes, I whisper questions to myself. Accepting that their sense of call is valid, are these persons the best and the brightest? Is that why God has called them and not someone else? Are they the most charismatic, the ones who will most effectively draw persons to their Lord? To be honest, some of them don't strike me that way. Would these persons rank highest on a vocational aptitude test? Or is it perhaps that they were simply the ones who responded to the sense of need? Were they, perhaps in some instances, a second choice, enlisted after God's higher draft choices decided to go with another team? I really don't know. You might even advise me that it's none of my business—not simply because it is primarily God's business, but also because what goes on in the interior of someone's soul is no one's business but his or her own. I concede as much. And yet, I wonder about the choice God makes in the call—while assuming that the person declaring the call testifies to a personal reality.

When Moses looked at Israel, he wondered, too, and this is to his credit. He makes a peculiar declaration, one in which he seems to begin a sentence that he then realizes is leading nowhere. He has just said that God has chosen Israel "out of all the peoples on earth" (Deut. 7:6). Now, it seems, he feels it necessary to explain why they have been chosen. Moses continues, "It was not because you were more numerous than any other people that the LORD set his heart on you and chose you—for you were the fewest of all peoples. It was because the LORD loved you and kept the oath that he swore to your ancestors, that the LORD has brought you out with a mighty hand, and redeemed you from the house of slavery, from the hand of Pharaoh king of Egypt" (Deut. 7:7–8).

Moses acknowledges that the predictable reason why God might choose a nation is because of its size. This reason doesn't apply to Israel, because they were "the fewest of all peoples." At the moment of Moses' presentation, Israel might have flexed her muscles and noted her count, but of course Moses' argument goes back to an earlier day. God had chosen Israel with the call of Abram and Sarai, when they were without children and Sarai was barren. That made them about as small as a nation could be! Even when the family of Israel moved to Egypt at Joseph's invitation, they weren't much—some seventy persons, just a good-sized family reunion. And when at last they were people enough to make a nice-sized city-state, they were slaves, a people with no promise whatsoever, firmly in the control of Pharaoh. They were, indeed, "the fewest of all peoples," by measure of numbers and by measure of their significance. So why then did God choose them?

Moses' answer: "because the LORD loved you," and particularly to fulfill the oath previously sworn to their ancestors (who were also a small people, as we have noted). I still remember the first time I became impressed with this passage. I was eighteen years old, the bass in a traveling male quartet. At the moment we were providing the music for a service in Tulsa, Oklahoma, where the speaker was reflecting on the fact that he felt twice-chosen, since he was a Jewish convert to Christianity. He spoke to us from the King James translation (the only translation generally available at the time), where the passage read, "The LORD did not set his love upon you, nor choose you, because ye were more in number than any people . . . but because the LORD loved you." "God loved you," the speaker said, "because he loved you." Quite without reason; quite beyond logic.

Two generations later, a biblical scholar reaches the same conclusion. Explaining Israel's role on the basis of Deuteronomy 7:8, J. Clinton McCann writes, "[I]n a word, this vocabulary is essentially about love."[1] It's an affair of the divine heart, and how does one argue with such a reason as that? Speaking of the human heart, Blaise Pascal said, "The heart has its reasons which reason knows nothing of." If we are compelled to accept the reasons of the heart in human affairs, how much more when the heart is divine?

A pragmatist might argue, of course, that God took the best of what was available. In the language of professional football, there are years when it's a poor draft for quarterbacks or tight ends. Has it been so with our human race? Leo Rosten, the Jewish author and social scientist, playfully responded to William Ewer's poem:

> Not odd
> Of God.
> Goyim
> Annoy 'im.[2]

Was it, perhaps, that of all this human race, the Jews were the most likely choice to get the job done, to be the ones who would convey not only remarkable concepts of the meaning of history, but more important, the understanding of God as One? And from a Christian point of view, was it, perhaps, that this was the people best equipped to be the channel by which God's Messiah would enter the world?

Again, from a very pragmatic point of view, God had to begin somewhere. On any project, large or small, one has to start with *some-one*. And one had better reconcile to the realization that all the some-ones are rather iffy choices.

In the case of the Jews, the choice has been a remarkable one. Mark Twain, who was not often given to sentimental statements, wrote in *Harper's* magazine over a century ago, "All things are mortal but the Jew; all other forces pass, but he remains. What is the secret of his immortality?" Half a century later, Adolf Hitler would put forth the greatest effort in history to extinguish a people, exterminating at least six million Jews from an already small population, but the Jewish people survived, making Twain's comment all the more insistent.

Whatever it is, Moses seemed to see it coming. "God loves you," he said, "because he loves you." It's very difficult to annihilate some-one with such credentials, and even more difficult to explain. The word is *grace*. Obviously, Moses knew something about the idea, even if he didn't use the word.

Chapter 9

One More Grand Chance

Scripture Reading: Judges 16:13–31

*W*hen I read the biblical story, I sometimes wonder at the kind of company God chooses to keep. I find this comforting, of course, because I don't consider myself a prime choice. Nevertheless, one notices that so many of the biblical characters seem unlikely vehicles for eternal purposes. And no one more so than that rough-hewn, one-man wrecking crew known as Samson, a judge of Israel.

Before going further I should probably clarify the term "judge." When we hear that term, we think of a rather dignified figure, often in a judicial robe and in some cultures also wearing a dusted wig. The judges in ancient Israel performed basic judicial functions, specializing especially in the kinds of matters that would today come before a small claims court. But the judges whose stories are told in the biblical book of that name were also executive officers, and it is their executive role that is emphasized in the stories in Judges and the opening chapters of 1 Samuel. They were often Israel's deliverers at those times when the nation had wandered from the divine covenant and had become enslaved to one of the enemy nations.

Some judges, like Ehud, were notable primarily for their derring-do (Judg. 3:12–30). Samuel was a spiritual leader, so that his home was not only the place where he "administered justice," it was also there that he "built . . . an altar to the LORD" (1 Sam. 7:17). Jephthah was admirable for his readiness to negotiate before going to war (Judg. 11:12–28); I see him as something of a statesman. But Samson? He seems a man ruled by his passions. There are two dominant, recurring scenes in his drama. In one, he is driven by his fascination with women—and as far as we can see, always the wrong kind of women. In the other, he is on a rampage of anger. He is constantly getting revenge for some real or supposed slight. But here's the astonishing part: God seems in every case to employ Samson's anger to purpose. That doesn't make the anger any prettier to behold, but it does add to the wonder of the continuing saga called Samson.

And yet, I have to admit that I find something appealing in this man. I think I would have liked him. The wife of a professional athlete once said to me, "Those of us who are married to athletic stars gradually learn that they can be slow to grow up. Most of them are loved and applauded from the time they're in middle school. They live in a world of unreality. Everything rides on one more touchdown or one more tackle. It's hard to grow up when you live in such a world." Samson lived in such a world, and as I read his story, I wonder if he never really grew up—until, that is, the day when he suffered his consummate defeat.

But I have to tell you something more about Samson. God seems to have liked him. Again and again in Samson's brief biography I find the recurring report that the spirit of the Lord came upon him. And it all began before he was born; indeed, even before he was conceived.

For forty years Israel had been under the control of the Philistines. The writer of Judges says that "the LORD gave them into the hand of the Philistines forty years," but judging from the usual pattern in the book of Judges, Israel managed well at getting into trouble unaided. Now the writer introduces us to a man named Manoah, whose "wife was barren, having borne no children" (Judg. 13:2). In the Bible, this sort of sentence is a way of announcing that excitement is on the way. Sure enough, an angel of the Lord visits Manoah's wife to tell her that she will conceive and bear a son. But there are stipulations. She is to abstain from wine or strong drink and any unclean food; and when the boy is born he will be under a Nazirite vow, by which a razor will never touch his head. Why? Because he is to be a special person, "who shall begin to deliver Israel from the hand of the Philistines" (Judg. 13:5).

So the woman bore a son, as promised, and named him Samson. He was special, no doubt about it: "The boy grew, and the LORD blessed him. The spirit of the LORD began to stir him in Mahaneh-dan, between Zorah and Eshtaol" (Judg. 13:24–25). The writer's careful identifying of the place has all the marks of a special religious experience. The classic stories of our experiences with God are identified with the places where they happened, whether it be Paul on the road to Damascus, St. Augustine in a garden, or John Wesley at a meeting place on Aldersgate Street. Places are made sacred and memorable by our God-encounters.

But Samson's conduct from this time forward doesn't reflect well on his religious experience. One day he sees a Philistine woman who appeals to him. He knows what he wants, and insists that his parents get her for him. When they resist, pointing out the religious and ethnic differences, Samson answers, "Get her for me, because she pleases me" (Judg. 14:3). One gets the feeling that Samson is used to having his way. Being an only child, he has not had to brook competition. I suspect that his parents catered to him also because of the divine endowments attached to his birth. The story that follows includes some showboating by Samson, a wager lost through deception by his wife, and an act of wanton violence, a demonstration of his extraordinary, reckless strength and his singular ability to deal with superior numbers.

The stories that follow add to the glamour of Samson's strength but to the discredit of his character. His sense of his rights is easily piqued, and he destroys with consummate energy and ease. There is no evidence of his being a person of worship or of godly commitment, yet the Spirit of God comes upon him in his times of need, and it is clear that the biblical writer wants us to understand that Samson's extraordinary exploits are not simply his athletic prowess; they are a gift from God. We tend to think of Samson as a steroid-muscular mountain of a man; a generation ago, Hollywood cast Victor Mature to fill his role. I think a case could be made for a Samson who was athletic—as was most of his world of outdoor physical laborers—but probably no more so than many of his peers. The most impressive thing about him was his hair. Year after year it grew, lush and full and crowning, and no razor touched it.

And the legends grew around him. He was just what the people of Israel needed. They couldn't really hope to compete with the Philistines in armed strength or international standing, but they could exult in their Samson's occasions of humiliating the enemy. As one who was pastor in Green Bay, Wisconsin, in the year when their beloved NFL team, the Packers, won one game, tied one, and lost all the rest, and who was still there a few years later when they won the world championship by defeating the New York Giants 37–0, I know something about what an athletic victory—especially one that humiliates the enemy—can do to a community's self-image. I repeat, Samson was just what Israel needed. They might not have a king or iron chariots, but they had Samson. And I suspect that if word got round about his moral peccadilloes, the people were inclined to shrug them off, as we sometimes do when the offender is our hero and is necessary to our own self-esteem.

And Samson had style, too. Three times in his short story he is pictured delivering a poem. He may be a wild man when challenged, but there's an aesthete here, too. Poet and novelist Phillip Lopate, evaluating Samson's foolish conduct with Delilah, says, "Any man who puts up with that many consecutive betrayals is not a tragic hero but a schlemiehl, a buffoon."[1] For those unfamiliar with Yiddish, *schlemiehl* is a person whose description includes such words as gauche, naive, gullible, or anyone who makes a foolish bargain. But Leo Rosten notes in his definition that a brilliant or learned person can still be a *schlemiel* (the spelling varies).[2] In his own way, Samson—as I see him—was a brilliant man, even though he played the fool. Sometimes, to use an old phrase, I think he was crazy like a fox. And when the writer of Judges concludes Samson's story, he notes that Samson had "judged Israel twenty years" (Judg. 16:31), which indicates that he fulfilled the day-by-day duties of his office in faithful fashion. And as I've already said, he was a poet.

But tragedy was pending, and Delilah was her name. The biblical writer tells us that Samson "fell in love with a woman in the valley of Sorek, whose name was Delilah" (Judg. 16:4). We're not told whether she was beautiful. We assume as much, but of course beauty is in the eye of the beholder, and anyone who has ever fallen in love can testify to the fact that this ecstatic experience has little to do with any conventional measures of beauty, intelligence, character, or worth. Whatever Delilah's attractiveness, apparently it did not include loyalty. As soon as the lords of the Philistines learned that Samson was seeking out Delilah, they presented her with an offer; if she could learn the secrets of his strength so they could overpower him, they would each give her eleven hundred pieces of silver. There is no indication that they had to raise the ante. She went right to work.

The scenario that follows is the reason for Lopate's contention that Samson was a born loser. When Delilah asked the source of Samson's strength, his first two answers were predictable and meaningless. But the third got closer to the issue of his life: Tie the seven locks of his head and make them tight with a pin, and he would be helpless. In each of these instances, Delilah did what Samson said, and each time when she announced, "The Philistines are upon you, Samson," he broke free with ease.

By now Delilah was tired of being toyed with. She responded as his wife-to-be had done years earlier, insisting that if he truly loved her, he would tell his secret. After days of Delilah's pestering and nagging, Samson "was tired to death. So he told her his whole secret" (Judg. 16:16–17). He had been "a nazirite to God" from his mother's womb; if ever his head were shaved, his strength would leave him and he would become as weak as anyone else.

As the biblical writer tells the story, Samson does, indeed, sound like a buffoon. A wiser man would have said, at some point, "I've been through this kind of dialogue before and look where it got me." Still more, he had to see that Delilah meant no good, and no matter how enchanting he found her—and I think her very insouciance made her still more compelling to him—he had to know that she would use whatever knowledge he gave her. He does, for sure, seem to be a *schlemiehl*, a buffoon, a pathetic fool.

But it's a familiar kind of fool, the kind we find in anyone who presumes upon his or her talent, standing, office, or power. If you think Samson a fool, you do so with justification; but recognize that he is a fool you have seen many times, in the world of politics, of sports, of business, of religion. Especially, perhaps, religion. Recognize that, given the right circumstances, you and I might be his kin. Samson was celebrating the arrogance of the privileged. He had enjoyed the touch of God's Spirit repeatedly. He had played at the edges of disaster and had always survived. It is so easy, under such circumstances, to feel invincible, and all the more so if you carry the feeling that you are called, that you are special. No wonder, then, that after he had revealed his secret and had fallen peacefully asleep after doing so, he thought to himself as he awakened, "I will go out as at other times, and shake myself free" (Judg. 17:20).

The Old Testament writers, particularly in such books as Genesis, Judges, and Jonah, show a lively sense of humor, but I don't think they intend to portray Samson as a buffoon. He is a man driven by his passions, and often given to rash decisions, but he has lived all his years keeping the vow driven into his being by his mother. Except for this: that he presumed on God. Indeed, he presumed on the grace of God, because he had been chosen without demonstrated qualifications, and had experienced the exultation of the spirit of God numbers of times—to the point, I think, where he assumed that he possessed the spirit and that he could exercise the power at will. He could, even, violate his vow and still shake himself free as at other times. Call him a fool, but not a buffoon. I think the biblical writer wants us to know just how ridiculous we are when we presume on the goodness of God.

If this were the end of the story, it would be a lesson in judgment, not grace. A New Testament preacher might see Samson as someone who committed the unpardonable sin, in his disregard for the God's spirit. Certainly Samson paid a fierce price. After Samson revealed his secret, the Philistines seized him without trouble. They "gouged out his eyes" and brought him to Gaza, where they bound him and set him like a beast of burden, grinding at the prison mill. The biblical writer tells us nothing of Samson's feelings. We don't know if he thought back on better days, though surely he must have. We're not told if he felt regret, though our hearts tell us so. Nor are we told that he repented of his arrogance and of the violation of his lifelong vows. Franz Wright, winner of the 2002 Pulitzer Prize in poetry, described the humiliation he felt when recalling his past as grace. "We are created," he said, "by being destroyed."[3] Was it so with Samson?

There was grace, no doubt about that. The biblical writer puts it succinctly. "But the hair of his head began to grow again after it had been shaved" (Judg. 16:22). Here is a gift. Not that his hair should grow again; that was natural enough. But it is a gift that the growing is significant. It doesn't change Samson's sin or the breaking of his vow. The vow is broken, and that is that. The hair was never to be cut, and it has been. That's the fact of it.

But grace is wonderfully unknowing of life's facts. The hair began to grow again. A sacrament is defined as "the outward sign of an inward grace." On that ground, let us call this story the sacrament of Samson's hair.

Since the writer bothers to tell us that Samson's hair was growing, we can only assume that Samson realized what was happening, and drew hope from it. So on the day when the Philistines called a religious festival, to celebrate the victory their god had given them in the capture of Samson, they took him from the prison to entertain them. Samson positioned himself for one last act of destruction, then called to the Lord. "LORD God, remember me and strengthen me only this once, O God, so that with this one act of revenge I may pay back the Philistines for my two eyes" (Judg. 16:28). Perhaps in earlier days Samson had not been so conscious that his strength came from God. Now he knows. He calls for revenge, a word that in itself can easily be dismissed; but consider also that it is a call for justice, a quality sacred to a fair God. And in that day, Samson won a greater victory than in all the rest of his life combined.

I suspect that all of us presume at times on the goodness of God. It seems like part of our human genetic code to do so. Some of us arrogantly misuse the gifts with which God has endowed us. And many of us—perhaps all of us—will confess that we have broken some vow made to God. I stand in awe that Samson's hair began again to grow. I marvel at the patient, unceasing reach of grace.

Chapter 10

Grace and God's Love for the Future

Scripture Reading: Ruth 1:1–5; 4:13–22

Now and then someone refers to the Old Testament book of Ruth as the greatest love story ever written. I'm never sure what they mean when they say this, but I'm always afraid they're referring to words they've heard recited in a wedding ceremony, sometimes by the bride and groom together, sometimes by the bride to the groom, and sometimes by a liturgist: "Entreat me not to leave thee, or to return from following after thee: for whither thou goest, I will go; and where thou lodgest, I will lodge; thy people shall be my people and thy God my God: Where thou diest, will I die, and there will I be buried: the LORD do so to me, and more also, if aught but death part thee and me" (Ruth 1:16–17 KJV). If this be the source of a person's identifying this book as an extraordinary love story, it's likely they also think these words were spoken between a man and a woman and not, as it happens, by a daughter-in-law to her mother-in-law.

Nevertheless, I agree that this is a great love story. It is, for sure, the story of a great love between in-laws, countering the image so popular of the latent hostility between mother and daughter-in-law. And eventually it is the story of the love of an older man for a young woman, and of her love for him. But far more than that, it is the story of God's love for our human race, beginning with the people of Israel, especially as this love is expressed in God's love for the future. As such, it is an expression of that particular form of love known as grace.

Before going further, let me say that grace, perhaps by definition, claims the future as its peculiar domain. Grace declares itself whenever the plot seems at a dead end. At that moment when it seems proper to write, "*Finis*," grace announces that there is a future. This is true whether grace is manifesting itself to a nation (as so often with Israel and perhaps with other nations in situations we haven't recognized), with a family (as in this story of Ruth and Naomi), and in individual lives (in stories too numerous to recite). This is the meaning of grace; circumstances say that night has fallen, and grace replies, "Morning has broken." Grace gives reason to hope; it insists that there is a future.

But let's get back to the story of Ruth. The book—no more than a short story—begins with shadows: "In the days when the judges ruled [if you've read the book of Judges, you know this is bad news], there was a famine in the land [this is trouble compounded. If war and inept leadership are not enough, now even nature is against us]" (Ruth 1:1). The situation is so bad that a man named Elimelech goes with his wife Naomi and their two sons, Mahlon and Chilion, to live in Moab. Economically forced migration can be painful enough under the best of circumstances, because it means leaving family, friends, and all that is familiar. But we know the situation must have been particularly serious when this family went to Moab, because there was an ancient enmity between the Moabites and the people of Israel; an enmity so severe that no Moabite was to be "admitted to the assembly of the LORD," even to the tenth generation (Deut. 23:3–6). Moab was a place an Israelite would go only if no other reasonable possibility existed.

Bad fortune dogged the family. First, Elimelech died. Then the two sons married Moabite girls. This must have troubled Naomi, since it violated still more dramatically their national alienation from Moab. But the worst was yet to come. By the time the family had lived in Moab about ten years, the two sons, Mahlon and Chilion, also died.

Now there were three widows, struggling for existence in a time and a culture that had no provision for widows outside of their families. Naomi heard that better times had returned to Israel, so she prepared to go back to her homeland, where the laws of family responsibility would give her some hope of support. She instructed her daughters-in-law to return to their mothers' homes in Moab, where they too would have some prospect of care. At first the girls insisted they would return with Naomi to Israel. But Naomi reminded them that there was no future in her. One daughter-in-law, Orpah, got the point. But Ruth clung to her mother-in-law, speaking the lines that since have been quoted as the essence of family loyalty; only death would part them, she vowed. So Naomi returned to Bethlehem, accompanied by her widowed daughter-in-law, Ruth.

Now the problem was survival. How could two widows keep alive in a world where women didn't work outside the home and where there was no structured welfare program? They became gleaners, following after the harvest workers. The system was spelled out in the Mosaic Law: "When you reap your harvest in your field and forget a sheaf in the field, you shall not go back to get it; it shall be left for the alien, the orphan and the widow, so that the LORD your God may bless you in all your undertakings" (Deut. 24:19). The same instruction was given for the harvesting of the olives and grapes.

And there was more. Israel had a system of economic redemption. It was built around the family structure and the responsibility of the extended family to care for their kin. If a family lost its property by natural disaster, by foreign invasion, by theft, or perhaps even by their own ineptness, the next of kin was required to restore the person's property or means of livelihood. This plan could include even marrying the widow of a relative. What this system lacked in romance it made up for in practical economics. This theme of redemption is a dominant feature in this book. Ruth has only 85 verses, but the Hebrew words for "redeem" or "redeemer" appear more than twenty times in that short compass.

So after we're told that Naomi had "a kinsman on her husband's side," a man who happened also to be prominent and rich, we have a feeling the plot is thickening when Ruth announces that she is going to glean "behind someone in whose sight I may find favor" (Ruth 2:2). She works industriously, and when the owner of the field, Boaz, comes to check on the progress of the harvest, he inquires about her. The Bible says nothing about Ruth's physical attractiveness; this is left to our imagination. Movie-driven as we are, we assume there are reasons why Boaz notices her. Boaz's supervisors explain that she is the Moabite who came back with Naomi, and that "she has been on her feet from early this morning until now, without resting even for a moment" (Ruth 2:7).

Boaz now speaks to Ruth for himself, asking her to glean in no other field, assuring her that he has ordered the young men not to bother her. Still more, he tells her that when thirsty she should "go to the vessels and drink from what the young men have drawn" (Ruth 2:9). Ruth thanks Boaz with great emotion. "Why have I found favor in your sight, that you should take notice of me, when I am a foreigner?" (Ruth 2:10). Perhaps Ruth's speech was only a formality, a soliciting of favor; I choose to see it as an overflow of gratitude from a woman who is painfully conscious that she is an outsider. She has been surprised by grace. Boaz doesn't allow Ruth to wallow in her unworthiness; he praises her for the loyalty she has shown to her mother-in-law. More than that, he recognizes her conversion to Judaism, as he prays that she will be blessed by "the LORD, the God of Israel, under whose wings you have come for refuge!" (Ruth 2:12).

Later in the day Boaz goes further still. He allows Ruth to eat with the reapers, then instructs his young men to let her glean among "the standing sheaves," and even to "pull out some handfuls for her from the bundles, and leave them for her to glean" (Ruth 2:15–16). That evening, when Ruth returns to her mother-in-law and reports on the day's exciting events, Naomi asks where she has gleaned. At the mention of Boaz, Naomi breaks into thanksgiving. "Blessed be he by the Lord, whose kindness has not forsaken the living or the dead! . . . The man is a relative of ours, one of our nearest kin" (Ruth 2:20). That is, he is a potential kinsman-redeemer.

From this point, the plot unfolds pretty rapidly. On the other hand, if the story were in the hands of a moviemaker, this is where the story would come into full orchestration. Naomi, the mother of all matchmakers, outlines a plan for Ruth. See where Boaz will be working this night, at the threshing floor. "Now wash and anoint yourself and put on your best clothes." Watch where Boaz lies down for his night's rest at the floor; when he is asleep, uncover his feet and lie there; "he will tell you what to do." Ruth has complete confidence in her mother-in-law's ancient wisdom. "All that you tell me I will do" (Ruth 3:2–5).

When Boaz awakens, and Ruth in the darkness identifies herself, Boaz is suddenly the suppliant. He sees her coming to him as an act of loyalty still greater than what she has already extended to Naomi, since she could have "gone after young men, whether poor or rich" (Ruth 3:10). But there is still an impediment. Another man in the village is a closer kin, with earlier responsibility (and privilege) in the redemption process; Boaz promises to take care of this matter in the morning.

And so he did. So they married, and lived happily ever after. But of course although the Scriptures rejoice in conjugal love and in human happiness, they set these wonders of life in the larger context of the purposes of God, which makes the wonders still more wonderful. When Boaz, in the company of the community elders at the gate of the city, completes the legal details of his role as kinsman-redeemer, he announces that he intends, in taking Ruth as his wife, "to maintain the dead man's name on his inheritance, in order that the name of the dead may not be cut off from his kindred and from the gate of his native place" (Ruth 4:10). When Boaz found Ruth at his feet on the threshing floor, he was an older man overwhelmed that a young woman would consider him for marriage; at the city gate, he is the "prominent rich man" fulfilling legal commitment to his kin. The line of Mahlon, son of Elimelech, will not be lost. You have Boaz's word for it.

So in good time, Boaz and Ruth had a child, a son. You will remember that I said earlier that the concept of the future is a major element in the meaning of grace, so we shouldn't be surprised that this union has a child; each baby, some sentimentalist has said, is God's vote for the future. But this baby is an especially significant vote for the future. For the women of Bethlehem, Naomi's lifelong friends who have loved her through many heartbreaking years, the baby is seen as God's kindness in providing that she has not been left without a next-of-kin. They bless their old friend with eloquent language of love: "He [the grandson] shall be to you a restorer of life and a nourisher of your old age; for your daughter-in-law who loves you, who is more to you than seven sons, has borne him" (Ruth 4:15). Though the words are extravagant, they are not casual. Almost any grandparent might seek a grandchild as "a restorer of life" because of the peculiar vitality a grandchild brings, but of course the writer means more than this. Naomi now has someone to carry on her line, thus restoring life to a line that had seemed, with the death of her two sons, to be extinguished.

The tribute to Ruth is as if a revival of religion had come to Bethlehem. The Israelites had been taught to despise Moab. It would have been enough for the village women to include Ruth in their feminine activities; for them to praise Ruth as better than seven sons ("seven" being the traditional number of completeness) was about as strong as praise could be. Our culture might see the words as a declaration of women's rights, and perhaps with some justification. But especially, here was an acknowledgment that God could find something good in an outsider, in a person beyond the family of Israel. It isn't surprising, then, that converts to Judaism often have been named Ruth in recollection of this remarkable Moabite woman. This, too, is a vote for the future, a millennial glimpse of the diminishing of ethnic and racial barriers.

But there is more. The biblical expectation of the future is more than wonderful but vaguely defined words like love, beauty, and goodwill. It is pictures: a lion lying with a lamb, children playing safely in the street, every family with its own vine and fig tree. And with all of that, the specific of a beneficent ruler—at first, David, and after that a descendant of David, the Messiah.

So the book of Ruth ends, not with our fairytale words, "happily ever after," a lovely phrase but short on concrete realities, nor even with Ruth and Boaz walking off into the sunset, hand in hand. It ends in a quite biblical way. First, there is the announcement about Ruth and Boaz's son, except that it isn't announced that way. Listen: "The women of the neighborhood gave him a name, saying, 'A son has been born to Naomi.' They named him Obed; he became the father of Jesse, the father of David" (Ruth 4:17). It's a wonderful scene. I wonder if some Jewish writer has made it into a Yiddish comedy? If so, why not? The generally second-class citizens of Bethlehem, this group of middle-aged and older women, have suddenly taken over; Boaz (rich and influential, and good, too) is in the background, and even Ruth. These women have announced that this is Naomi's baby, and who is going to argue with them? This is a baby born to a woman who had lost her line of descent, and it came by way of a Moabite girl, blessed be God! When there is no future, there is grace.

Then the writer of this wonderful vignette does a very Old Testament kind of thing. We think the story is over, but he wants to make the point clear. He does so with a genealogy: "Now these are the descendants of Perez: . . . Boaz of Obed, Obed of Jesse, and Jesse of

David" (Ruth 4:18, 21–22). It may seem prosaic to us, but it is a very anthem of victory. This story that began in the dark days of the judges, with famine, emigration, death, and hopelessness, ends with Israel's greatest king. This is grace, as demonstrated in God's love affair with the future. It is a story for anyone who thinks his or her story has already ended.

Chapter 11

A Directory of Grace

Scripture Lesson: 1 Chronicles 1–9

I owe something to Lloyd Outland, so I must mention his name. Lloyd died at least forty years ago, and since neither he nor his only sibling had any children, there's no one left to celebrate his name, but by the very nature of what I am about, I wouldn't dare to omit it.

Lloyd was a retired business executive, a member of a congregation I served so long ago, and our across-the-street neighbor. One early evening he crossed the street in particularly resolute fashion. Someone in our church office had misspelled his name in a church mailing, and he wanted to make sure that I both corrected the error and realized what a misdemeanor had been committed. He explained that he had been a lifelong employee of Dun and Bradstreet, and that they had taught him that nothing is more important to a human being than the person's name. "It is the only sure possession anyone has," he said. "No one legitimately can take it from you. It means more than your credit reference or any college or university degree. A person who misspells your name has committed the ultimate insult, because they have violated you at the level of your most sacred rights."

His speech was both eloquent and earnest enough to convince me, but the shame is that I needed any such convincing. By that time I was not only a seminary graduate and a pastor of some years, but more important, I had read the Bible through from beginning to end a dozen or more times. In doing so, I had encountered (and I suspect, had complained about) the long lists of names in the Bible. Like the section of 1 Chronicles that I've designated as a Scripture reading for this chapter, a section I don't really expect you to read. But I do want you to hold the pages between your fingers for a moment—long enough to sense their sacredness. Beneath their possible tedium of reciting, beyond the difficulties of pronunciation, catch their sacredness. And ponder that in this and all other such biblical listings there is an expression of divine grace.

We twenty-first-century people aren't immediately ready to appreciate the significance of names. When we pay our utility bills or our credit card accounts, we're warned that we ought to include our account number with our payment. Our income tax payments get their certainty via our Social Security number. The numbers on our driver's license, our order form, our plane reservation—all of these have pushed our names in the shade of significance. Communication via the Internet seems at times to have eliminated the use of names; first it was the elimination of the courteous greeting "Dear"; now many communications begin without the mention of a name. The writer assumes you know the message is for you; otherwise, why would it be in your e-mail inbox?

The trivialization of names has carried over into the world of commerce, though with a peculiar twist. A new corporation, or the merging of several corporate bodies into a new entity, usually involves an expert in naming. The corporation must have both a name and a logo that will "sell," that will capture attention, and that will stay in memory. But these new names rarely have character, and even more rarely carry the name of a person or a family. The name of a commercial institution is now more often a series of letters than the name of an individual or a partnership of individuals.

I contend that we are poorer for this; immeasurably poorer. When the Social Security program came into existence, some imaginative preachers saw the Social Security number as the mark of the beast (Rev. 13:16–18), warning their congregants that without this number they soon wouldn't be able to buy, sell, or do business. The number is no mark of the beast, but it has contributed to the beastly practice of marginalizing names. Government and commerce have combined to replace our names with numbers. Mind you, I see the convenience of it, and in some cases even the necessity, but I'm troubled by the trend. A number is impersonal, while a name—whether formal and given by ceremony, or a nickname, given by instinct—is the essence of who a person is. A number is a convenience, in which the person is subservient to the system; a name belongs to the individual and is more important than the convenience of any system. Some will object that they don't like their name; nevertheless, the name acknowledges one's tie to the rest of humanity, whether by family name, by adoption, or by ceremonial bestowing. And of course one can change a name, legally, to establish a preferred identity. But the name matters. I recall a bishop who, while proud of his role and title, objected to being addressed simply as "Bishop." He felt that substituting his office for his name diminished him as a person. I suspect he was right. We are a name before we are titles, office-holders, or vocations, and we will be names after the other identifications are outdated or denied. Shakespeare paid tribute to the unique, peculiar value of a name when in *Othello* he said that the person who "filches from me my good name . . . makes me poor indeed," but with his robbery does not enrich himself at all.

The Bible—especially the Old Testament—cares about names. In truth, "cares" is too weak a term; the caring is a kind of passion. No grand declarations are made, but the sheer prevalence (the Bible mentions more than three thousand persons by name), the anecdotes around some birth names, the renaming of persons in the course of their spiritual journey, and the blessings and curses related to names all add up to an awesome case for the inestimable worth and significance of our names. The Psalmist, in an intense prayer for vengeance, calls for many judgments on his enemies, but nothing worse than "may his name be blotted out in the second generation" (Ps. 109:13). When the Bible leaves a person without a name, one has a feeling that the writer intends either to emphasize the lack of standing the person has (as in the story of the woman of Samaria, in John 4), or to indicate that the person wasn't as significant as he thought himself to be, as in the story of the rich man and Lazarus, where the rich man is left anonymous while the beggar is identified by name.

It seems likely that most biblical persons got their names as we do, sometimes by virtue of a name passed on from generation to generation and sometimes, no doubt, simply because of its euphonious appeal to one parent or the other. But some persons got names because of particular circumstances at their birth. Esau was given a name that described his physical appearance, while his twin brother, Jacob, was named for a peculiar incident at birth—a name and an incident that became associated with his personality and character (Gen. 25:24–26). Jabez was named for the pain his mother experienced at his birth (1 Chr. 4:9–10), and Ichabod for the news of military and spiritual disaster that apparently speeded up his coming to birth (1 Sam. 4:19–22). But every name was considered sacred, and an aim of one's life was to be held in such respect that the reputation one had would bless one's name. So the writer of Proverbs said, "A good name is to be chosen rather than great riches" (Prov. 22:1). And while one might think the word "reputation" could be used here rather than the basic word for name, it is probably significant that the same Hebrew word is used for both purposes. Rightly so, because one's name is inseparable from the record attached to it. So someone says, after being falsely accused in the public media, "They've ruined my name."

The book of 1 Chronicles begins in a fashion that seems abrupt to my kind of mind. "Adam, Seth, Enosh; Kenan, Mahalalel, Jared" (1 Chr. 1:1–2). The plotline looks thin! The writer doesn't bother to tell us what he's about, why he has started where he has, or where he's going. And so he continues, through several thousand words. Occasionally he interrupts his directory with a succinct biographical sketch. Nimrod "was the first to be a mighty one on the earth" (1 Chr. 1:10). One child was named Peleg because "in his days the earth was divided" (1 Chr. 1:19). Some items make one wonder what anecdote the writer may be alluding to, as when in giving his list of "the kings who reigned in the land of Edom before any king reigned over the Israelites" he says of Hadad, "the name of his city was Pai, and his wife's name Mehetabel daughter of Matred, daughter of Mezahab" (1 Chr. 1:43, 50). At the least, the ancient writer left a name whose sound must have pleased Don Marquis, the early twentieth century newspaperman, poet, and playwright, who gave us Archy and Mehitabel, the legendary cockroach and alley cat duo.

So what is the writer of 1 Chronicles about? How does he dare to begin with nothing more than a recital of names, offering no explanation, and continuing in what seems to us to be an interminable fashion?

Let's begin with the pragmatic. It's pretty clear that the Chronicles were written after Israel had returned from the Babylonian and Persian captivity. It was crucially important that the people regain their sense of national identity. There had been some intermarriage and some assimilation of the ideas and practices of their captors. I suspect some of the Israelites had begun to be comfortable with the Babylonian and Persian ways of life, including no doubt some of their pagan practices. They needed to know who they were. They needed also to know who they were not. This lengthy genealogy answered both questions. They were, for one thing, a people who sensed that their history was linked to the very existence, as they understood it, of the human race. Their story began with Adam.

But they have their distinctions. They look back to Seth, Abel's replacement, not to his murderous brother, Cain. And though the descendants of Ham and Japheth are briefly mentioned, the story settles quickly on Shem. Then it becomes more particular. Isaac has twin sons, and the writer tells us a little about the line of Esau, because they, too, are blessed of God. But beginning in the second chapter, the story centers on Israel in general and on the tribe of Judah in particular. This emphasis makes clear that Israel has a unique role in the story of the human race, and that Judah is central to that role; the household of David, son of Jesse and family of Judah, is key to the story.

We think we could get along without some of the names. The chronicler knows better. And he is so confident of the importance and rightness of what he is doing that he sees no need for a rationale, no necessity for explanation. "Adam, Seth, Enosh": where else would you begin if you were about the magnificent business of reminding your people of their divinely historic role? And all the more, when your people have been subjugated for some two generations by nations that are militaristically more powerful, but who lack—from Israel's point of view—the role of divine destiny. Israel identifies itself with the whole human race, then particularizes itself as uniquely significant to that race.

There's the pragmatic case, with its profound spiritual significance. But I see more than that. The case could have been made other ways—ways more pleasing to the average reader. The chronicler might have turned poet, singing of a nation's unique role. Or he could have done it philosophically and theologically, constructing an argument with its own intricate logic.

But not so, because this is a biblical writer, and the biblical writers love names. Even when these writers are making philosophical and theological points, they do so by telling stories about people. Their beliefs are rarely set in abstract language; they come to us via persons—men and women, heroes and villains, blessed and cursed. So the writer of Chronicles gives us names, including a section where he lists the musicians that ministered before King David. Persons matter, and a sure way to show that they matter is to mention their names. The writer of Chronicles couldn't have done better if he had been trained by a veteran reporter on a major metropolitan newspaper: "Get the names, and be sure of the spelling. People don't want their names misspelled."

And what does that have to do with grace? Just about everything. The Bible is, of course, theology, the study of God. But running second, and sometimes a surprisingly close second, the Bible is anthropology, the study of our human race. That's because the kind of theology the Bible offers is a theology that emphasizes the exceeding importance of humans. It suggests that God doesn't want the divine story told without including humans.

Now that's important in its own right, but it would still leave many of us feeling lonely. We don't want to be lost in the crowd. It's nice to know that God loves the whole world, but what about *me*? And if some tough-minded philosopher tells me to get over it, that it's the human race that matters and that I have only drop-in-the-bucket significance, I have to answer that I can't get over it, because I'm human—and to be human is to be self-conscious, and to think I have some worth. I have to know that it matters whether I live or die.

The romantic in me thinks it's significant that each of us has fingerprints, footprints, and voice prints uniquely our own; indeed, that we have a genetic code that will identify us from only a small particle of the body. We think it's the Creator's way of saying that each person is singularly important to God. The psalmist said that we are "fearfully and wonderfully made" (Ps. 139:14). The scientist now says "Amen" with our DNA.

But I want to see it in writing, and that's where those opening chapters of 1 Chronicles—and dozens of similar, shorter passages—come in. The Bible gives us names. Thousands of them. Each one says that the individual matters; to be specific, that the individual *is* individual. Nothing shows this better than a name. Anyone who has ever searched a list outside a high school teacher's door, to see if he or she has made the team, the play, the choir, or the literary society knows how much a name matters. At such a moment, nothing is more beautiful than one's own name.

I'm an insistent underliner. If you look through my personal library, you can tell how far I've gotten into the book by the underlining. I suspect I would know whether or not I wanted to buy a book if the reviewer would tell me how many lines have been noted in some way. So I apologize that I've underlined very little in the first nine chapters of 1 Chronicles. I suspect I should underline every name. You can be sure I would underline Ellsworth Kalas if it were there.

Still more, I should write beside each name, *grace*. Adam, grace. Seth, grace. Enosh, grace. An astonishing directory of grace. I think Lloyd Outland would understand. But only if the names were spelled correctly.

Chapter 12

New Every Morning

Scripture Lesson: Lamentations 3:19–33

*L*ife is marked by crises but it is lived by the day. Some crises come like a declaration of war: the loss of a job, the severing of a friendship, or the doctor's call for major surgery. Others may be so lovely that we hardly think of them as crises—the day of someone's birth, the first day of school or the first day on a new job, or the purchase of a home—but they are crises nevertheless, because they shape or challenge life in strategic ways. Even when the issue is something we have anticipated and planned for, like the purchase of a home, our response can turn the anticipation into distress. Such days take on a kind of mythic quality, so that ever after we use them as reference points for other life events, as when we say, "This happened just a week after Jimmy was born," or "I met this fellow the day I registered at the university."

But though we mark our lives by such crises, we live them out by the day. The crises are really relatively few. They gain their prominence by the smallness of their numbers. Those unfortunate people who seem to live their lives from one crisis to another eventually choose the larger crises as life's time posts. Most of life, however, follows rather regular, ordinary patterns; and yet it is these regular patterns that determine the skill with which we meet the crises.

The short, unrelenting Old Testament book known as Lamentations is a crisis book. According to tradition, the prophet Jeremiah wrote Lamentations at the destruction of Jerusalem in 586 BCE. More recent scholarship suggests that Jeremiah was probably not the author, not only because the style of writing is unlike that in the book bearing his name, but also because he may have been in Egypt at the time of the destruction. But while the author may be anonymous, the occasion itself and the reason for the book's existence are without question.

An attack on a nation's capital is a thrust into a people's very heart. The harm is far more than its measurable economic and military significance; it violates a nation's very essence. It is the trampling of ten thousand flags, the desecrating of a people's history and identity. But for the Jews it was still more, because Jerusalem was not only the capital, and not only the city of David, Israel's most beloved king. It was the city where the Lord God was pleased to dwell. So a poet would write later, "If I forget you, O Jerusalem, / let my right hand wither! / Let my tongue cling to the roof of my mouth, / if I do not remember you, / if I do not set Jerusalem / above my highest joy" (Ps. 137:5–6).

So when the Babylonians, with their dominant military machine and their superior economic resources, marched into Jerusalem, they left in shambles not simply walls of security and public buildings, but the *raison d'être* of a people. Worst of all, the Babylonians destroyed the temple, the nation's proudest piece of architecture and the symbol of her relationship with God. At the least, this destruction was an act of physical blasphemy; at the worst, it suggested that perhaps God was inadequate against the Babylonians, or even worse, that God did not care.

How do you respond at such a time? You call upon your poets. I dare to venture that as long as humans have faced devastation, they have sought poets to assuage their grief and to restore their spirit. The lines may be a ditty that the soldiers sing as they march, or a call to arms to be quoted from platform and pulpit, but there will be words for the occasion, and poets will provide them. Some may say that they know nothing about poetry and don't care to learn, but in a crisis they lay hold of the words the poets have written.

I repeat: we don't know who this poet was. But whoever it was, it was a person—or perhaps even persons—who wrote from the passion of national and personal pain. Scholars point out that the writer employed the Hebrew lamentation meter that is known as the "elegiac meter," which by its structure carries the sound of sobbing. We lose that quality in the English translation, but the language the poet employs needs little help to convey the sense of utter desolation.

It is as if the poet were taking us on a guided tour of destruction:

> How lonely sits the city
>> that once was full of people!
> How like a widow she has become,
>> she that was great among the nations!
> She that was a princess among the provinces
>> has become a vassal.
>
> (Lam. 1:1)

But the poem has another quality, an almost incongruous one. It is as carefully constructed as an exquisite needlepoint. The first two lamentations are made up of three-line stanzas, with the first word of each unit beginning consecutively with the twenty-two letters of the Hebrew alphabet, and the fourth follows the same pattern but with two-line stanzas. The third lamentation is more emphatic in its style; it, too, has three-line stanzas, but each line of a given stanza begins with the particular letter of the alphabet. The fifth lamentation is not alphabetized, but it has twenty-two lines, corresponding to the number of letters in the Hebrew alphabet.

At first this careful structuring seems almost incongruous. Can one organize pain? Indeed, is it even right to do so? Should pain, perhaps, be allowed simply to express itself in incoherent groans? Perhaps the answer is in poetry that deals with another kind of powerful emotion: love. Many of the most moving sonnets (as with Shakespeare and Elizabeth Barrett Browning) have been composed as love poems. If "I love you" is beautiful in its own right, I suggest that it is still more beautiful when the lover invests the artistry to speak the love in measured lines and cadences. So, too, pain deserves some sort of literary embrace. A crude man may curse, but a saint will weave grief into a holy tapestry.

One of the most moving lines is spoken as if it were coming from the city itself:

> Is it nothing to you, all you who pass by?
>> Look and see
> If there is any sorrow like my sorrow. . . .
>
> (Lam. 1:12)

Here is the sense of forsakenness. Jerusalem has been destroyed, and no one cares. No one rises up to defend her; no sister nation comes to her assistance. Pain shared is pain relieved, but there is no such opportunity for Jerusalem. No one chooses even to notice her pain, or even to speak of it, let alone seek to cure it. With such the case, there is no sorrow like this sorrow.

But of course if Lamentations were nothing but inconsolable grief, it would have no place in this book. There are anthologies where it would fit admirably; both its artistry and its subject matter would guarantee that. But our message is grace. Why do I place this book in a study of grace?

Near the middle of the poem, celebrating the Hebrew letter *Heth*, the poet declares what he knows about the character of God. Now let it be understood that the poet believes that the disaster Israel has suffered is a judgment from God. The Babylonians may be the delivery agent, but this is "the rod of God's wrath" (Lam. 3:1). No matter:

> The steadfast love of the LORD never ceases,
>   his mercies never come to an end;
> they are new every morning;
>   great is your faithfulness.
> "The LORD is my portion," says my soul,
>   "therefore I will hope in him."
>   (Lam. 3:22–24)

Another poet at another time (traditionally said to be David), reflecting some of the same human struggles, celebrated the same divine quality:

> Weeping may linger for the night,
>   but joy comes with the morning.
>   (Ps. 30:5)

Life has its crises, and because of their sometimes arrogant strength, they claim higher status in our calendar. But life is lived out by the day. "This, too, shall pass." The line was ancient when Abraham Lincoln quoted it in a speech in 1859, but his further commentary is worth remembering. These words, he said, are "chastening in the hour of pride," and "consoling in the depths of affliction." The poets both in the Psalms and in Lamentations were laying claim to the assurance that what they were enduring would pass.

To think so as a general principle is noble and optimistic, but it may also be without foundation. But of course the writer of Lamentations was not offering a facile optimism, and he would have been astonished that anyone might think his convictions were so poorly founded. His confidence was in the character of God. He was counting on "steadfast love," "mercies," and "faithfulness"—qualities that would not have occurred in the religious views of the peoples and nations adjoining them.

I wish I knew the name of the person who wrote this declaration of faith. Of course my wish is rather foolish, because if a name were attached to the words or to the book of Lamentations, I wouldn't really know any more than I know now. Still, when someone has left behind such words as "the steadfast love of the LORD never ceases," I want to attach a name to him or her; I want, by using a name, to feel I know this person. I wonder how it is that he could believe that God's mercies are new every morning. A day or a week before, when the invading armies destroyed Jerusalem, God's mercies seem to have lapsed. How could this writer conclude, in the face of such a holocaust, that tomorrow would be full of mercy, and so too all the tomorrows following? The events of their recent history would have seemed to argue otherwise.

Several generations ago believers spoke not only of *faith* but also of *staith*. They were thinking of the quality of believing that is steadfast; it *stays*. It is faith, yes, but with a certain dogged quality that will not let go. Such was the faith of the lamenting poet. It was a faith with a basis as much in the justice of God as in the goodness of God. Indeed, at the moment of writing, justice was the predominant mood. In anger, God had "destroyed Israel," but for the poet, this was right and proper. It was a reason why God could be counted on. God's character was constant; evil was equally evil in God's sight, whether performed by Babylon or Israel. God's love for Israel was not of such a nature that Israel's misdemeanors would be acknowledged with a shrug of the shoulder. The character of God was constant. God was just, no matter who the people in question.

And because God was constant in justice and judgment, so God could be counted on to be constant in mercy, in steadfast love, in faithfulness. If God's mood varies in matters of justice and judgment, how can we expect that the other facets of God's character can be depended upon?

So it is that the poet can move from the horrific pain of a city spoiled to the grand expectation of tomorrow. He sees a constancy in God that gives utter certainty to tomorrow. On this basis, he knows that God's mercies "are new every morning." These mercies will not be exhausted; they will endure because of the source from which they have come. As an Israelite, he remembers his nation's experience in their wilderness wandering, when each morning they found a new supply of manna for the day. God's mercies, he reasons, are like that; as surely as a new day comes, there will be this manna of mercy awaiting my taking.

It is the day-by-day quality of this mercy that impresses me most. As I said earlier, crises mark our calendars, but they do so because they are the exceptions of life, the intrusions. The poet knows that mercy is not an intrusion and it is not an exception. It is, of all things, a marvelous commonplace. It is "new every morning." Still, though I call it a commonplace, it is not ordinary. The mercies are *new*. See the calendar, note the date. Now look at the mercy. It is not last year's mercy, or even yesterday's; it is new this morning.

This is a compelling fact. On some yesterday, Jerusalem's walls fell and the temple was destroyed. But life must go on. The poet has to arise this morning, no matter what happened yesterday. And so it will be tomorrow, and the day after tomorrow. And he will, because there will be new mercies this morning, tomorrow, and every morning.

I think the poet who wrote Lamentations knew more about the daily mercies of God than a poet who lived, say, when the walls of Jerusalem or its temple were being built. I certainly wouldn't minimize the joy of achievement; I'd rather preach for the dedication of a new church building than to preside on a Sunday after a building has been destroyed by fire or flood. Nevertheless, I believe the poet of Lamentations knew more. I'm sure he had experienced God's sustaining grace in blessed days and uneventful ones, and I trust he had thanked God at such times. But in the midst of desolation he was learning a new thing, a surprising thing. God was as present in the devastation as in the day of obvious favor.

Students of preaching agree that Arthur John Gossip, a Scottish preacher who lived through the last quarter of the nineteenth century and the first half of the twentieth, preached a sermon in 1927 that will always rank among the greatest. It was the first sermon he preached after the unexpected death of his wife. In the course of the sermon he confessed, "I do not understand this life of ours. But still less can I comprehend how people in trouble and loss and bereavement can fling away peevishly" from their faith. "In God's name," he cried, "fling to what?" Then he went on to say, "You people in the sunshine may believe the faith, but we in the shadow must believe it. We have nothing else."[1]

Is this a testimony of despair? Hardly. It is the witness of one who has looked in the face the worst of days and has been sustained. While doing so, he has also observed that some persons, at such a time, have no sustaining. And still more, that what he has is enough, and more than enough, and that it has a strategic beauty of its own.

And best of all, this person knows that there will be a fresh goodness tomorrow, and tomorrow, and tomorrow. God's mercies are "new every morning." When the writer of Lamentations made that discovery and gave that witness, he had hold of grace.

Chapter 13

Grace in an Iron Band

Scripture Lesson: Daniel 4:10–15, 24–27

*C*hautauqua County in western New York State likes to boast that it gets more snowfall than any county in America. I was ready to believe the boast on a January day in 1967 as I followed a real estate agent through mountains of snow to look at a summer cottage. A cold, forsaken summer cottage doesn't look very attractive in January, but it struck me so favorably that I completed the purchase that day before it was time for the afternoon train that would take me back to Cleveland, Ohio.

A few months later, when our family saw the cottage without the setting of snow, we discovered there was a great old tree stump just in front of the porch. It had sometime been sawed off within six inches of the ground. Now, almost directly in its center, there was a tiny sprig of a tree, not more than six or eight inches high.

Summer walkers on that street made a conversation piece of the tiny tree in the stump. They speculated about how a seed could find root in the stump. How long would it be, they asked, before the stripling would die? Some poetic souls suggested we should name the cottage for the sprig from the stump—perhaps "Resurrection House" or "Renewal Cottage."

Personally, I always leaned toward naming it "Nebuchadnezzar's Place." As I sat on the porch on lazy summer days, enjoying the casual reading I couldn't pursue during the rest of the year, I would look at the tiny tree that asserted itself ever more insistently each year and I would think of Nebuchadnezzar, fabled king of the Babylonian empire.

Secular history has a good deal to say about Nebuchadnezzar, but the story I want to talk about comes from the Old Testament book of Daniel. Nebuchadnezzar was near the height of his storied career when he had a strange dream. In it he saw a tree so powerful that its height seemed to reach to heaven and its impressiveness to the ends of the earth. But a heavenly messenger said, "Cut down the tree and chop off its branches, / strip off its foliage and scatter its fruit" (Dan. 4:14). The animals that had once enjoyed the tree's shade would flee, the messenger said, and the birds would forsake its now destitute state.

Obviously the tree was in a hopeless state, not only cut down but its branches chopped off, its foliage stripped and its fruit scattered. *But.* "But" is one of those good news–bad news words. When it comes in the midst of a pleasant story you fear what will follow. In the midst of bad news, however, "but" has an upbeat sound. So it is here. "But leave its stump and roots in the ground, / with a band of iron and bronze, / in the tender grass of the field" (Dan. 4:15). The tree's story has not ended. Not only will its stump and roots remain in the ground, the stump will be held together with a band of iron and bronze.

The trees of this world are always being cut down. History is full of such decimations. These cuttings seem so often to come when a tree is at its grandest state. I have no idea who first said, "The bigger they come, the harder they fall," but no folk wisdom is more certain. It applies to the world of sports, of politics, of professional religion, of corporate grandeur. The bigger the tree, the grander its reach, the more impressive its stature, the more desolate will be its collapse. Nebuchadnezzar's dream (a nightmare sort of dream, really) is fulfilled every day—indeed, every hour of the day—at some level or another of human life.

In the book of Daniel, the cutting of the tree was an act of divine judgment. In a sense, it always is. I'm not suggesting that God announces at frequent intervals, "Bring out the saw and the ax; now the arrogant one is going to get his due." In the case of Nebuchadnezzar, the cutting was ordered by heaven. As I see it, there is a factor in all the cuttings of Earth's forests that is by heaven's order; in some cases, like Nebuchadnezzar's, directly, but in most cases indirectly. That is, I think judgment and justice are built into our universe and that they proceed their unerring way without specific divine direction.

Sometimes the judgment is more surely aimed but mostly it is the inevitable process of our own doing. And when I say "our own doing," I don't mean that the judgment always comes singularly to the guilty party. We are all bound up together in the bundle of life, so that none of us lives or dies simply to himself or herself. The good I do has a fallout of benefit to others, and the evil I do inevitably hurts others as well as it hurts me. In fact, sometimes it may hurt others more than it hurts me, which only underlines the demonic nature of evil.

As a whole, the pattern of divine judgment pleases me. I favor justice and I am profoundly grateful that God, according to my biblical understanding, is a God of justice. I hate terribly that the judgment that falls on a dictator (whether political or corporate) brings pain on so many innocent bystanders. But since the blessings that come through good people benefit so many who have made little or no contribution to the goodness, I can't complain that the system cuts both ways. Again, this is both the price and the benefit of living in a community, including communities we haven't necessarily chosen.

But the thing I like best about God's structure of justice is this: there is still a place for grace. In Nebuchadnezzar's dream, grace is conveyed in an image: the tree is cut off but a stump remains. Yes, and more than that: the stump is held together "with a band of iron and bronze." The one who has ordered the cutting has also ordered preservation. The quality of this preservation is as sturdy as could be imagined by an ancient mind; the stump is held together by a band of iron and bronze.

The dream troubled Nebuchadnezzar. I suspect it troubled him all the more in that in the middle of the report, the heavenly messenger began referring to the tree as "him" rather than "it," which is a little like the doctor moving from a third-person statistical report on an illness and speaking specifically of "you." The messenger in the dream said, "Let his mind be changed from that of a human, / and let the mind of an animal be given to him. / And let seven times pass over him." "It" is now "he," and Nebuchadnezzar knows that he is the he. All of this was decreed so that "all who live may know / that the Most High is sovereign / over the kingdom of mortals" (Dan. 4:16–17).

Something about this dream made the king sense that it was, as Dickens might have said, more than a bit of undigested beef. The king's wise men couldn't explain the dream, so he called on his Jewish counselor, Daniel. Daniel loved Nebuchadnezzar. He wanted no evil to befall him, so he hesitated to interpret the dream. This dream was something, Daniel said, that he wished would happen to the king's enemies rather than to the king. The tree represented Nebuchadnezzar. He had prospered so that the whole earth seemed to take comfort in his shadow. But he had become proud and arrogant and now judgment was going to come upon him. Like the tree, he would be cut off; cut down to the very ground. Daniel then did a bit of preaching. He appealed to the king to atone for his sins "with righteousness," and to extend "mercy to the oppressed, so that your prosperity may be prolonged" (Dan. 4:27).

If Nebuchadnezzar bought the sermon, it was for only a limited period of time. I understand this, not only because in my years of preaching so many of my sermons have been effective with some of my hearers for only a limited time but worse, because sometimes they've been so short-termed even for me, the preacher. As for Nebuchadnezzar, he found it hard to think poorly of himself when his public relations staff (which included everyone in the king's court) continually told him how great he was. One needs a very sensitive conscience to hear the quiet voice of the Holy Spirit when the corporate board has just raised your compensation by seven figures, or you've won reelection by an overwhelming margin. After twelve months the king was walking on the roof of the royal palace of Babylon and said, "Is this not magnificent Babylon, which I have built as a royal capital by my mighty power and for my glorious majesty?" (Dan. 4:29). The king's thoughts were not without foundation. During Nebuchadnezzar's rule the city of Babylon became one of the most beautiful cities of the ancient world. It was probably Nebuchadnezzar who built the "Hanging Gardens," one of the seven wonders of the ancient world. He had reason to look out and feel very good about himself.

But "[w]hile the words were still in the king's mouth," the voice of judgment announced that he was to be banished from human society, becoming like an animal, until seven years had passed by. And the judgment fell immediately.

Most judgments don't fall with such immediacy. Most of the time, it seems to me, judgments come so gradually or by such logical course that we may not easily see that they are judgments at all. They seem to be nothing more than the logical course of events. And as I said earlier, in a sense they are nothing more than logic. We sow a certain kind of seed and we can expect a certain crop. God's judgments are ultimately as predictable as a farmer's routine. If as individuals and societies we believed in this holy logic, a great many of history's tragedies would never occur.

But there was nothing gradual about the judgment that came to Nebuchadnezzar. While the words of arrogance were still rolling sweetly in the king's mouth, the divine sentence was passed and Nebuchadnezzar entered a darkness of insanity. I think the prophet is suggesting that arrogance and pride are always only one step short of insanity. Sometimes this is clear, though we usually see it better in other people than in ourselves; and when we see it in ourselves, we do so some considerable time after the plot has unfolded.

The king was so deranged that he "was driven away from human society, ate grass like oxen, and his body was bathed with the dew of heaven, until his hair grew as long as eagles' feathers and his nails became like birds' claws" (Dan. 4:33). And so it was for seven years; seven, the biblical number for completeness, for a finished project. And with seven years of such isolation from the human community, the king was indeed a finished project: "I, Nebuchadnezzar, lifted my eyes to heaven, and my reason returned to me" (Dan. 4:34).

I knew it would turn out this way. I knew it when I saw that judgment left a stump with roots in the ground, and when the stump was embraced by a band of iron and bronze.

That picture has encouraged me so often in the pastor's study. I have sat nothing less than hundreds of times across from some stump of a life. Their physical appearance has not often reminded me of Nebuchadnezzar in his wild state, though now and then a drug addict or a career alcoholic has come close. Usually, however, the stump is inside, and at first well hidden. There are a few minutes of pleasantries (the kind Nicodemus was counting on when he greeted Jesus with, "Rabbi, we know that you are a teacher who has come from God"), then the stump is unveiled. I remember a man who was in the usual litany of his complaints about the church when suddenly he said, "I know I'm an unpleasant person. I hate the way I am. But I don't know how to be any different." And the college student, as pretty as a nineteen-year-old dares to be: "I'm just so unhappy! I hate myself for the mess I am inside." Or the woman who has just, in my presence, received the oncologist's terminal estimate: "three to six months, at best." As soon as her doctor left, she had a stump report for me. "It's because of my sins. I'm being punished for what I've done."

It's then that I think of a pagan king, a man as well known in the Scriptures for his arrogance as in secular history for his regal achievements. I remember that when life was most full of promise he was peremptorily cut to the ground. But there was a stump, with roots, and God ordered that it be bound with iron and bronze. A pagan king got grace. He didn't know the name for it, nor did Daniel, it appears. But Daniel knew how to draw it even if he couldn't spell it.

Such grace ought to, of course, be followed by a change of conduct. It was so in Nebuchadnezzar's story.

> Now I, Nebuchadnezzar, praise and extol and honor the King
> of heaven,
>> for all his works are truth,
>>> and all his ways are justice;
>> and he is able to bring low
>>> those who walk in pride.
>
> (Dan. 4:37)

I am impressed by the king's declaration of faith. He praises the truth and justice of God, though it is that very justice that has given him seven years of ugliness. And he praises God's power for bringing low "those who walk in pride," though he is the one who has just undergone this humbling process. He's a new person, as changed as was Saul of Tarsus after his shorter and less terrifying trip. I don't know what Nebuchadnezzar did with his newfound way; secular history gives us no report, and even the book of Daniel abandons the story without any sequel. And as it happens, that's enough for my present purposes, since I wanted simply to talk about the wonder of Old Testament grace without pursuing a full theology of redemption.

I said earlier that life's judgment process brings tragedy not only to the person who has sinned but also to innocent bystanders. No tree falls in the moral forest without a sound. Judgment seems an equal opportunity operator. Its fallout strikes rich and poor, male and female, young and old, talented and obscure. Death comes to all our dwellings, and sickness to most of them. Few of us escape some betrayal by friend or family and still fewer the inner ravages of defeat. At such times and occasions a good many of us are sure that only a stump remains. We're sure we'll never win again, never be well again, never be loved again.

Go to Nebuchadnezzar's place. The tree may be cut very close to the ground, but there are still roots. And if you look closely, you will see a band of iron and bronze. Call it grace. Daniel drew the picture even if he didn't know the word.

Chapter 14

Indomitable Grace

Scripture Reading: Job 42:1–6, 10–17

*T*homas Carlyle knew something about biography, loving it so much that he considered it the only real expression of history. Being so devoted to biography, Carlyle knew as much as anyone about heroes. In his study of heroes, early in the nineteenth century, Carlyle chose the book of Job in a chapter on "The Hero as Prophet," describing the book as a "Noble Book; all men's Book! . . . There is nothing written, I think, in the Bible or out of it, of equal literary merit." When Robert Gordis, then of the faculty of the Jewish Theological Seminary of America, wrote his study of the book of Job, he quoted Carl Cornhill, who described the book of Job as "one of the most marvelous products of the human spirit, belonging like Dante's *Divine Comedy* and Goethe's *Faust*, to the literature of the world."[1]

I'm sure I sound audacious when I venture a still stronger opinion, but I submit that Job exceeds both *Divine Comedy* and *Faust* as "products of the human spirit," not only because it has held its place in the marketplace of ideas much, much longer, but also because it has extended its influence over a much wider community of readers and listeners. Dante and Goethe appeal to a rather select audience. Job, somehow, cuts through all classes and conditions of our human race, from simple to sophisticate. The uneducated, nineteenth-century slave preacher made Job come alive to his audience; the contemporary university lecturer explores Job with a circle of graduate students. Job seems to move effortlessly from one audience to another.

The book of Job is about that most painful philosophical enigma, God, humanity, and evil. But its power is that in the book of Job the enigma is wrapped up in a person. One can discuss philosophy anti-septically, while pouring still another cup of coffee or knocking the ashes from a pipe. But there's nothing antiseptic about Job. As we read his story, then engage with him in the sometimes accusing, some-times angry, sometimes defensive dialogues with his friends, we find we can't remain in the bleachers; we are thrust into the game. Unbid-den, we come alongside Job. We wonder why his friends can't see his case; and when at last God visits Job, we're ready at times to chal-lenge God on Job's behalf when Job will not.

Because in some measure or other, Job is every person. I have known only a few persons whose lives were as completely decimated as Job's. I think of Horatio G. Spafford, author of the hymn-poem, "It Is Well with My Soul." After he lost four daughters at sea, later his wife, and then his considerable wealth, most of his Christian friends decided that he must be a sinner, else all these troubles would not have come upon him. Most of us, however, get our troubles in smaller por-tions and generally distributed over a longer period of time. Never-theless, in our troubles we're inclined to that self-centered but very human question, "Why me?" When we do, we feel akin to Job. From Job's troubles to ours may be a philosophical stretch, but we make the connection.

Is there any grace when everything seems against us; and worse, when it looks as if God is not only distant but perhaps part of the problem?

You remember the Job story. He was "the greatest of all the peo-ple of the east" (Job 1:3). He had reason each day to look out on his vast holdings, his beautiful family, and his community prestige and sing, "O, What a Beautiful Morning!" Life could hardly have been better. But he was not simply a successful man, he was a truly good human being. The biblical writer says that he was "blameless and upright, one who feared God and turned away from evil" (Job 1:1). In fact, this is the first thing we know about him after being told his name and address. He was also an admirable family man. He wanted so much to pass his faith on to his children that when they celebrated he would "rise early in the morning and offer burnt offerings" for them, fearing that they might "have sinned, and cursed God in their hearts" (Job 1:5). This man seems good all the way through.

But suddenly Job is a pawn in a game between God and Satan. God boasts of Job's virtue, and Satan charges that this virtue is surface stuff that has never been put to a test. So Job, innocent and helpless, loses his wealth and his family in a series of irrational disasters. When Job is resolute in the face of loss, God reminds Satan that Job "persists in his integrity" (Job 2:3), so Satan raises the ante: see what Job will do when he loses his health. Job loses more than his health. His wife does not turn against him, but finding his pain more than she can handle, she urges him to curse God and die. When his friends arrive, they sit in silent sympathy for seven days, then—to Job's pain but to our eventual enlightenment—they begin talking. Their basic conclusion is quite simple. God is just, so what happens to us humans is just. If we are good, we prosper; if we are bad, we suffer. So, in converse, if we're suffering, it's because we're bad. Ergo, since Job is suffering, he must be bad. Indeed, considering the extent of his suffering, he must have been *very* bad. Perhaps the worst of his badness was that it was so well hidden that no one knew the extent of his evil.

Job's three friends, and eventually a latecomer, Elihu, make their case eloquently. As the discussion develops, they become vehement, especially when Job insists on defending himself. Job is impassioned throughout. The discussion may be philosophical with his friends, but for Job it is existential. He's drowning in trouble, so any tenuous lifeline is crucial.

Job refuses to impugn the character of God though at the moment all of the evidence seemed to cast God in very questionable light. As Archibald MacLeish puts it in his play, *J.B.*, a twentieth-century adaptation of Job's story,

> If God is God He is not good,
> If God is good He is not God.[2]

If Job operated from the reasoning of his friends, he would begin singing that playful, cynical little tune with MacLeish's character. But whatever evidence to the contrary Job encounters, he is certain of the character of God. At the same time, however, he insists on his own innocence.

If grace matters in the sunshine, it matters still more in the dark. And of course no darkness is more irreversible than a darkness that seems to represent God and to be God-sent. At times, Job wavers. If he did not, we could only conclude that he has lost his senses or that the portrayal is a fraud. He asks why God contends against him.

> Does it seem good to you to oppress,
>   to despise the work of your hands
>   and favor the schemes of the wicked?
>   (Job 10:3)

He confesses that he loathes his life, and more than once he wishes that he might die. The worst of his pain is that there is no one to plead his case with God:

> For he is not a mortal, as I am, that I might answer him,
>   that we should come to trial together.
> There is no umpire between us,
>   who might lay his hand on us both.
>   (Job 9:32–33)

And yet, with all of that, Job still will not give up his confidence in the character of God or in his own innocence. He examines his conduct, his truthfulness, his care for his slaves, his relationship to the poor. In matters of sexual integrity, he anticipates the teachings of Jesus in the Sermon on the Mount, insisting that he has "made a covenant with [his] eyes," so that he would not "look upon a virgin" (Job 31:1). In his last speech before the extended declarations from Elihu and God's eventual confrontation, he is concerned above all else that he might be "false to God above" (Job 31:28). But above all, he wishes still,

> Oh, that I had one to hear me!
>   (Here is my signature! Let the Almighty answer me!)
>   Oh, that I had the indictment written by my adversary!
> Surely I would carry it on my shoulder;
>   I would bind it on me like a crown;
> I would give him an account of all my steps;
>   like a prince I would approach him.
>   (Job 31:35–37)

Ill fortune, whatever its form, is hard enough to bear. It is almost unbearable, however, when we're given the impression that God wants it so. The well-meaning person who counsels the sufferer by saying, "It is God's will" has solved a problem by making a larger one. Now the character of God is in question, or at least God's wisdom; why would God do such a thing? Or else our own character: "This has come on me because I deserve it." Sometimes, of course, this is true. A good many of our troubles are self-inflicted. But Job refuses both ideas. He insists that God is just, and he is equally sure that his own way of life is free from sin.

Grace has many faces. John Newton testified, "'Twas grace that taught my heart to fear, / and grace my fears relieved." It was grace that prepared him, Newton reminds us, for a fuller experience of grace. Or in the language of theology, we have to meet prevenient grace before we can find saving grace. I submit that Job's experience demonstrates the *sustaining* power of grace. He will experience the grace of God when at last his fortunes are reversed, but meanwhile he must survive. He must keep heart until rescue comes, because rescue won't matter if he is no longer there to receive it. Something must keep Job holding on.

A humanist would call it the indomitable human spirit. I'm not one to minimize this quality, but I feel something more is present in Job's case. I say this, not out of my religious prejudices, though I readily admit that I am prejudiced on the side of God and faith. I say it because it is consistent with Job's character. Job was a person of such insistent goodness that he feared nothing more than that his children might inadvertently displease God. His success and prosperity somehow had not soured him with arrogance. I repeat what I said earlier: Job was a truly good human being. So, now that he had lost wealth, position, family, and health, and now that his friends seemed set on demolishing what little was left of him, Job had only this, the grace that had blessed his life through all of his halcyon days. Now that grace was sustaining him.

But grace isn't finished. Job has wanted to have an audience with God. Now God grants it, indeed, commands it.

> Then the LORD answered Job out of the whirlwind:
> "Who is this that darkens counsel by words without knowledge?
> Gird up your loins like a man,
>   I will question you, and you shall declare to me."
>
> (Job 38:1–3)

Job had complained earlier that God was not a man, so he could contend with him and present his case; now God answers that this is a court where a human voice can be heard. He is to gird up his loins "like a man"; it is as a human that he will be accepted and will get an audience.

But in truth, Job doesn't so much get an audience as become one. God begins a dramatic interrogation: Where were you when I brought this universe into creation? Have you commanded the morning? Do you know the springs of the sea, the dwelling of light, the storehouses of the snow? Do you understand the mysteries of rain, the movement of the planets, the action that turns clouds into floods of water? Job takes an overpowering excursion through nature, with each scene punctuated by a query calculated to convince him that he is rather small stuff.

But it is not a merciless declaration of divine power. Rather, it is God's assurance that Job (all of us Jobs!) has nothing to worry about. If God can manage a creation from Earth's foundation to the storehouses of the hail, from Pleiades to the birthing of a mountain goat, can God not be trusted with Job's fortune? And if God's approach is so emphatic as to seem like overkill, perhaps it is God's way of indicating the absurdity of our fears. Job gets at least part of the point. "See, I am of small account; . . . / I have spoken once, and I will not answer; / twice, but will proceed no further" (Job 40:4–5). But God isn't done. There is another call to gird up the loins, and a further excursion through creation. Now Job goes a significant step further. It isn't simply a matter of his insufficiency; that outlook is soon unproductive. Job acknowledges the greater fact, that "no purpose of yours can be thwarted"; and with that, a moving witness:

> I had heard of you by the hearing of the ear,
>   but now my eye sees you;
> therefore I despise myself,
>   and repent in dust and ashes.
>
> (Job 42:5–6)

Job, the remarkably good and sensitive man, has come to a new understanding of God. He now has a firsthandedness about his relationship that was not there before.

But the story is not over yet. In fact, it's here that we pick up the plot that we pretty much left behind in chapter 3, when we got into the philosophizing between Job and his friends. Now Job's world begins to be set right. First, God rebukes Job's friends: "for you have not spoken of me what is right, as my servant Job has" (Job 42:7). I venture the friends were shocked to hear this, because they had seen themselves as God's particular defenders. Herein lies a lesson for us all.

Then the writer tells us that "the LORD restored the fortunes of Job" (Job 42:10). With a flourish!—twice as much as he had before. And again, he has sons and daughters, but with a note that is significant: the daughters are identified by name, they are described as the fairest in the land, and they receive an inheritance along with their brothers. Job lives another one hundred and forty years, "and saw his children, and his children's children, four generations" (Job 42:16).

There's a kind of primitive, fairytale feeling to all of this, a "they lived happily ever after" quality. Its naive simplicity seems strange after the philosophical journey we have taken in the long body of the book. It's as if the writer were saying, "You thought these questions were terribly complicated, didn't you? But see how simply it all turns out? God wins, and true righteousness wins. In the end, that's all you need to know."

It is as if the writer were giving us a kind of child's view of heaven. Satan, who was so prominent in the first two chapters, is conspicuously absent. God sees no reason to boast of Job or to declare victory; the evidence speaks for itself. Goodness has triumphed, and all is well; indeed, extravagantly well.

And there was grace all the way. A kind of tenacious grace, which kept Job going, and grace extended by God so that whatever was temporarily lost during Job's trials is now restored, in an in-your-face manner. There is an indomitable quality in grace, a quality that reflects grace's roots in eternity. That indomitable quality took residence in Job.

Chapter 15

Songs of Dis-grace

Scripture Lesson: Psalms 3; 38

Some words and their opposites seem entirely unrelated, as if they were born in different times and places and grew up in different neighborhoods, only to find one another later in life. These are words like love and hate, truth and lie, good and evil. But other words and their opposites are first kin. They give one the feeling that the good concept was already so well established that its ugly opposite decided to identify itself by claiming association with the first. I speak of such words as honor and dishonor, tasteful and distasteful, welcome and unwelcome, grace and disgrace. Especially, *grace and dis-grace.*

I wonder who first coined the word *disgrace*? Whoever it was, he or she was a natural theologian. Somehow I feel that the word was not used, at first, by a professional wordsmith—not a member of what we now call "the chattering classes." It was not a theologian, a philosopher, a journalist, or an essayist. It could have been, of course; I can't prove my point. But somehow I feel the word was first used by, perhaps, a mother who is frustrated to the point of frenzy by the misconduct of her offspring. How can she show the degree of her distress? "You are," she says, her voice now dropping to a whisper, "You are a—*dis-grace!*" And from there, the theologians, philosophers, and essayists picked it up.

But it's no fun to be in a situation of disgrace. To be in grace is to be accepted, regardless of merit; to be in disgrace is to be shut out—and again, regardless. I have no idea how early we become acquainted with disgrace, but I know that we experience disgrace long before we can speak the word. Our pulse, our blush, and our kidneys define it

109

before we can find it in a dictionary. I suspect that our knowledge of disgrace begins the first time someone says, "Shame on you," because shame and disgrace are very close kin. The kindergartner who is shut out of a game or a conversation stands alone in *disgrace*; judgment has been passed, and he has been cut off from society. On the other hand, the old schoolroom punishment of making an offender stand in the corner was sometimes counterproductive; the offender knew that for some of his classmates, his role of isolation was a compliment to his audacity.

Some people, in the pain of unremitting disgrace, turn to drugs or alcohol; some, even, to suicide. Now and then we read a tragic news-paper report of someone who, accused of a crime, takes his own life in the jail cell, sometimes to protest innocence and sometimes to acknowledge guilt, but always to confess disgrace. It's the loneliness of disgrace, the being cut off, that so eats at the human psyche. I won-der what made William Shakespeare write, "When in disgrace with fortune and men's eyes / I all alone beweep my outcast state."[1] As is so often true of Shakespeare, he got the point exactly: it is this matter of "men's eyes," and being "all alone" and in an "outcast state." Put those elements together and you have sketched the profile of disgrace. It is the judgment of "men's eyes" that makes for disgrace, because disgrace is a judgment passed by others. So Sophocles wrote, "In dark-ness one may be / ashamed of what one does, without the shame of disgrace." It is our nature as social creatures that makes us susceptible to disgrace. Thus we may feel guilty about an unworthy thought, but there is no disgrace unless those thoughts are somehow made public.

So, too, it is because of this social factor that the punishment of disgrace is the feeling of being alone, and in an "outcast state." The old proverb "Misery loves company" is true in all sorts of circum-stances, but particularly in those where disgrace makes one an out-cast. The incontinence that sometimes comes to the elderly is less painful in a nursing home than in the world outside because it does not make one an outcast in the nursing home. The disgrace of a fail-ing grade is less painful when a third of the class is in the same boat.

The book of Psalms has so many songs of disgrace, or so many songs where disgrace is a contributing theme. The frequency of this theme reflects the importance of community to the Israelites. Where our culture glories in the individual and in individual rights, theirs centered on the community and one's place within the community. Thus, whatever isolated one from the community was supreme punishment. Obviously, we aren't immune to this issue, but we're more likely to assume bravado: "If they don't like it, that's their problem." The Israelite, so bound to community, knew better than to strike such a pose. They knew disgrace was not so easily ignored, nor was it easily remedied. A contemporary public personality can hire a public relations firm to change the public perception of his or her persona, with carefully planted news items and subtle altering of appearance and style. The ancient world had no such devices. True, someone close to the king could have a runner go before his chariot, announcing, "This is a man whom the king favors!" But the average person was the helpless object of word-of-mouth reports. Come to think of it, the Internet may restore this form of communication to first place. Where an old-fashioned gossip needed half a day to reach a few friends and neighbors, the Internet gossip, aided by Internet friends, can reach thousands within hours. And in a peculiar way, with more authority than newspaper or television: "I got this from a friend, and he got it from his sister." Disgrace may be entering a new era of empowerment.

So the Israelite turned to God, especially through the psalms. We often note that in most of the Old Testament, God speaks to us, while in the book of Psalms we humans speak to God. Mary Ellen Chase says that this is because of the "tenacious, unshakable assurance" the Hebrews had in their God and "because of their faith in His purposes for them as His people and for all mankind."[2] I always marvel at the candor with which the psalmists spoke to God about the affairs of their lives. They were altogether sure that what was happening to them was of interest to God. Long before Jesus said, "And even the hairs of your head are all counted" (Matt. 10:30), the psalmists were telling God the slights and pains of their lives, both great and small. Well, they were right. What seems an amusing bump in the road in retrospect was a mountain when we first encountered it. The psalmists had the good sense to know that if something matters to us, it matters to our caring God. And somehow they didn't think God required a long view from us, with its philosophical outlook. The long view comes later; pain is now.

So the psalmist told God how people were treating him.

> O LORD, how many are my foes!
>   Many are rising against me;
> many are saying to me,
>   "There is no help for you in God."
>   (Ps. 3:1–2)

Do you see the strategic pain? It is not simply that the writer has enemies; after all, who can hope to live without critics, distractors, and
perhaps even some who wish our demise? But some of these enemies
are passing judgment on his relationship to God. They are taking him
from the realm of grace to that of disgrace.

There is pain in any conflict, but few pains are more poignant than
those in which religion becomes a weapon. Obviously, no one is in a
position to evaluate another person's relationship with God, but this
fact doesn't seem to deter us from doing so. This is what makes religious controversies so mean and so difficult to deal with. When the
profane say, "Damn you," it doesn't matter much, because the person
using the oath doesn't profess ecclesiastical authority. But those who
say, "You're out of the will of God," or who insist, "I've prayed about
this [which suggests that you have not, or that if you have, you probably haven't heard well], and you're in the wrong"—then it is difficult
to reply. Not many of those with whom we associate are likely to say,
"There is no help for you in God"; they say, rather, "All I want is what's
best for the church" (translated: "You do not"), or "The next generation will know how wrong you are" (that is, "God is on my side").

If, as tradition says, David wrote Psalm 3 as he was fleeing from
Absalom's revolt, he had to confess that his enemies had a pretty good
case. David had betrayed his nation and his God as well as his family in the Bathsheba affair; if ever there is any justification in suggesting that someone is out of favor with God, David's enemies had
evidence. And David, on the other hand, had reason to see himself in
disgrace. Indeed, all kinds of disgrace! What worse, than to have your
son strike a coup for the family business, especially when the family
business is a throne; and worse, still, when the son is the kind of hand-
some, able fellow who might have caused people to say, "He'll be better than his father someday."

And if David's disgrace was not complete in Absalom's uprising, a pesky, minor character, Shimei, completed the shame. Shimei was part of the extended family of the late King Saul. It appears that he had resented David for years, and now that David was in ignoble retreat, Shimei took advantage of the chance to mock him, cursing him and throwing dust and rocks on him as David fled the palace. Shimei's language could easily have formed the basis for the prayer in Psalm 3: "The LORD has avenged on all of you the blood of the house of Saul, in whose place you have reigned; and the LORD has given the kingdom into the hand of your son Absalom" (2 Sam. 16:8). If David was reflecting on this experience later that night, he had reason to say, "[M]any are saying to me, / 'There is no help for you in God.'"

A word must be said for learning from the experiences of disgrace. Specifically, to what degree have I brought this disgrace on myself? Might I have prevented such ignominy if I had conducted myself differently? Any time one prays for deliverance from disgrace one ought to ask what part repentance should play in the prayer. Sometimes the issues of disgrace are entirely out of our control; sometimes we are victimized, whether by the judgment of others or by adverse turns of fortune. But sometimes our conduct aids and abets disgrace. In any event, we should search the soul, to see what we can learn. This is not easy counsel, because when one is in the clamorous pit of disgrace, the normal mood is self-pity. Self-pity is also self-deceiving; we need to challenge it.

I remember a woman long ago who was afflicted with what her generation somewhat delicately referred to as a "social disease." Her husband had been guilty of an infidelity, and had brought the disease to her. Someone had told her that Psalm 38 was describing just such a situation, except that the writer was the guilty party, rather than an innocent victim. The woman saw a description of her physical condition in the psalmist's words:

> [T]here is no health in my bones
> because of my sin.
> For my iniquities have gone over my head;
> they weigh like a burden too heavy for me.
> My wounds grow foul and fester
> because of my foolishness;

. . . .
For my loins are filled with burning,
   and there is no soundness in my flesh.
               (Ps. 38:3b–5, 7)

And then there was the disgrace that came from the disease:

My friends and companions stand aloof from my affliction,
   and my neighbors stand far off.
. . . .
For I pray, "Only do not let them rejoice over me,
   those who boast against me when my foot slips."
. . . .
I confess my iniquity;
   I am sorry for my sin.
               (Ps. 38:11, 16, 18)

I have no idea if the woman was right in connecting the words of the psalmist with her circumstances. I can see why she thought so; these were wounds that would "foul and fester," causing loins to be "filled with burning," and they were, indeed, because of someone's "foolishness." And no doubt (especially in that more sensitive time), friends and companions would "stand aloof from [the] affliction," and "neighbors [would] stand far off." Whatever a scholar would say about the connection, as a pastor I empathized fully with her use of the Scripture to her comfort. In her own mind, she was in disgrace, and in this psalm she found grace. If the Scripture described a circumstance akin to her own, then her shame was uniquely within the boundaries of Scripture. I affirmed her trust.

The psalmists were not the only Old Testament writers who dealt with disgrace. Nehemiah felt it when enemies laughed at his efforts to rebuild the walls of Jerusalem: "Hear, O our God, for we are despised" (Neh. 4:4). Surely we have to infer a feeling of disgrace for Hosea when his wife turned to whoredom, and for the prophet Jeremiah when he felt that the very God whom he served was mocking his efforts. And who was more surely in disgrace than Job—sick, destitute, bereft of family, condemned by his friends. In every case these persons were shut out by some portion of society, and in some instances they felt, at times, shut out from God. This is the nature of disgrace; whether guilty or not, we are isolated and rejected. Sin may or may not be a factor in disgrace; its primal characteristic is simply ostracism. Disgrace is a leprosy where it is unnecessary for its victim to cry "Unclean"; others cry it for us.

But in all these Old Testament instances where a person was suffering disgrace, the victim dared to turn to God. They possessed the quite irrational confidence that God was concerned about what people thought of them. Mind you, these were persons with a high view of God, who saw The Holy at work in nature and in history, a God who was involved with the business of nations. But they were sure God also cared that someone wagged a head at their condition, or shot out a lip in scorn. They reported these embarrassments to God with the kind of details your neighbor might use when recalling for you an indignity suffered in the shopping mall. They were very sure that all of this mattered to God.

Then, too, perhaps their attitude was shaped in part by the conviction that no other opinion mattered if only they could enjoy God's approval. What matter is the judgment of a human court, if the eternal court counts us innocent? Perhaps it was such a sublime confidence that sustained them. If so, it was a right one.

Call me petty if you will, but I'm glad the Old Testament saints left behind such a picture of God. Because all of us sometimes find ourselves in situations of disgrace; sometimes because we have courted it, and sometimes because it has pursued us. At such a time, I am strengthened to know that there is grace to deal with my disgrace.

Chapter 16

Better than We Can Ever Deserve

Scripture Reading: Psalm 103:1–14

*M*ost of the time I don't really need to know who wrote a given psalm. Some devotional writers say that the point of the Psalms is not the circumstances in which they were written but the way they speak to our particular circumstances. This is probably an overstatement, but there's truth to it. And of course the scholars have a point when they say that in those instances where a superscription identifies a specific incident, it is not necessarily so; that these superscriptions are tradition and not part of the original text. Still, I tell myself that the tradition is the oldest data available to us regarding writer and setting, so it's worth something. At the least, it gives our imaginations a frame within which to draw its pictures. So it is that I want, now and then, to know why it was that a given writer wrote as he or she did. I tell myself that perhaps I would understand the passage at a more per-sonal level on the basis of knowing something about the person who wrote it. And because the psalms are inherently so personal, such knowledge helps one get the feeling of a psalm (or any other writing) as well as its stated content.

So I wish I knew the circumstances for Psalm 103. But all we have is that brief line: "Of David." Someone bothered long ago to tell us in other instances that David wrote "when he feigned madness before Abimelech" (Ps. 34), and other such identifying lines; why not tell us something more about this Psalm, which contains some of the most heartrending lines to be found anywhere in all of literature. Why did tradition tell us nothing? Well, that's the way it is, so we have to make the best of it.

But who would write something like the following, and why would he or she write it?

> The LORD is merciful and gracious,
>   slow to anger and abounding in steadfast love.
> He will not always accuse,
>   nor will he keep his anger forever.
> He does not deal with us according to our sins,
>   nor repay us according to our iniquities.
> For as the heavens are high above the earth,
>   so great is his steadfast love toward those who fear him;
> as far as the east is from the west,
>   so far he removes our transgressions from us.
>   (Ps. 103:8–12)

These are the thoughts of someone who knows something about sin, and who considers himself more than a garden variety sinner. His is no passing formality of penance. He feels that God has a perfect right to be angry with him, so now that he feels forgiven, life seems to him to be showered with blessing. He can hardly find language to express it. How great is God's love? Something beyond measure, like the distance separating the heavens from the earth.

I don't run into many people who have such a sense of gratitude for sins forgiven. In truth, I don't find very many who are seriously concerned about their sins. Sometimes, if the sin is cast in psychological terms so they understand it as a personality deficiency rather than a theological state, they may show concern about a remedy. But in such instances they're more likely to look for therapy rather than divine forgiveness. One might conclude that a good many of us live in a sin-free world, since we know so few persons who are concerned about their sins or who feel so ecstatic about being forgiven.

But the author of this psalm was serious about sin and forgiveness. How come, and if so, can we perhaps learn something from him? If, as the superscription says, this is a psalm of David, it's easy to speculate on what might have driven him. Since sex is the primary preoccupation of our culture, we are quick to reason that this psalm probably relates in some way to David's adulterous relationship with Bathsheba, and to the murder that followed. Ancient tradition associates Psalm 51, that most moving penitential cry, with this event. Anyone who reads that psalm finds it easy to make the association. The writer's agony of remorse is appropriate to such a breach of goodness.

I like to think of Psalm 103 as a sequel to the David/Bathsheba story and the experience of repentance in Psalm 51. There's no tradition to substantiate my theory; it just seems logical to me. After all, from an evangelist's point of view, Psalm 51 is incomplete. We know the sinner repents, but we don't know that he has been accepted. Psalm 51 says nothing about the joy of sins forgiven; rather, it is a continuing expression of regret with repeated appeals for forgiveness. There are promises that when his sins are forgiven, he will rejoice, but the sense of forgiveness is missing. With this fact in mind, Psalm 103 speaks to my imagination. I see David, some days or weeks after his meeting with the prophet Nathan, finally grasping the wonder of grace. His sin had been enormous, so enormous that he feared God's Holy Spirit would be taken from him. Now he knows he is forgiven. He had said, "[M]y sin is ever before me" (Ps. 51:3). But now, no more! Now he exults, "[A]s far as the east is from the west, / so far he removes our transgressions from us" (Ps. 103:12). The holy contrast makes this psalm the exquisite sequel to Psalm 51, the completion of the act of divine acceptance.

Perhaps it was so. If David did indeed write this psalm, it's hard to imagine a more satisfying scenario than to connect it with the Bathsheba story. But making this connection plays too easily into our common definitions of sin. And come to think of it, our common definitions leave little room for what has been classically referred to as "the seven deadly sins." If our times give sin any place in our thinking, it tends to be at the headline level. We see sin, if we see it at all, as the most egregious violations of moral conduct, with little thought for the sins of the mind, the tongue, and the spirit. So we calculate, with hardly a thought, that if someone is carried away with the sense of sins forgiven, it must be someone guilty of particularly heinous transgressions.

But it isn't necessarily so. Your sins don't have to rate the front page in a scandal sheet to evoke profound relief with the experience of forgiveness. Consider Charles Wesley, cofounder with his brother John of the Methodist movement. He was born into a Christian home, his father an Anglican priest and his mother, if anything, even more devout than his father. When he studied at Westminster School, he soon became head boy, a proper tribute to his disciplined ways. When he had the opportunity to live with a rather well-to-do relative in Ireland, he chose rather to be a student and eventually a lecturer at Christ Church College, Oxford. In his pursuit of true piety, he organized what we today would call a small group, but one far more disciplined than most of us would ever consider. They called it the Holy Club, but other students referred to them as "Methodists," because they were so untiringly methodical about their search for God. Like his brother John, Charles came to the Georgia colony in America as an Anglican priest, and, again like John, failed there and returned to England.

But things went well for him on his return to England, well enough that he had reason to think the world was his oyster. He was privileged, by selection, to present the Oxford Address to King George II, and to dine with the king the following day. But Charles was not a happy man. He was religious, but he sensed himself a sinner. On Sunday, May 21, 1738, however, in a small gathering in his home he had a religious experience. "I found myself at peace with God, and rejoiced in hope of loving Christ."

How will such a person describe his conversion? Son of a devout household, circumspect to the point of priggishness in his conduct, a scholar by instinct and training, already ordained to the Christian ministry: how will he feel about his sins, if any? Two days after his religious experience, Charles wrote a poem:

> Where shall my wondering soul begin?
> How shall I all to heaven aspire?
> A slave redeemed from death and sin,
> A brand plucked from eternal fire.
> How shall I equal triumphs raise,
> Or sing my great deliverer's praise?

This is the language of someone whose new course of life must be radically different from his old. Obviously Charles thought it to be so. In a second verse, he wondered how he could tell the goodness of God that made it possible that "I, a child of wrath and hell, / I should be called a child of God." Someone who writes like this—"A slave redeemed from death and sin, / A brand plucked from eternal fire," "a child of wrath and hell"—clearly sees himself as a full-orbed sinner. Nor was this simply an early response to a dramatic religious experience. Charles pursued this theme and mood in many of his hymns in the years that followed. He spoke often of God's power to save "harlots and publicans and thieves," and often in a way that suggested he considered himself one of their company.

How is it that a person who had lived a quite sheltered life should think himself so fortunate to be saved? Some would explain his thinking by the theology in which he was raised, and they would have a point. But not enough of one, especially in light of the essential agnosticism that pervaded England at the time. I would attribute at least part of Charles Wesley's attitude to a high level of self-awareness. He recognized that though he was a morally upright person, he was quite capable of something else. He thanked God in one of his poems that he had not been one of the "young corrupters," but confessed that it was because of his "sacred cowardice"—the sort of social restraint that has kept many of us in paths of what was once known as middle-class morality. I submit that Wesley was grateful not simply for deliverance from sins already committed, but also for deliverance from the far more obvious sins he knew himself so capable of committing.

But there is more; and whatever the author of Psalm 103 had in mind, I'm sure this further element was a factor. The issue with a forgiven soul is not so much the enormity of a sin committed, but the crisis of one's relationship with God. Paul Tillich, the twentieth-century philosophical theologian, saw sin as alienation from God, and God as the ground of our being. I doubt that the psalmist would have thought of God in such philosophical language, but he would have known the reality to which Tillich referred. To be cut off from God is to have the very ground taken from beneath us. There is no longer a place to stand.

This sense of the importance of God is not something that all persons feel all the time, however, so the alienation that comes with sin is not so pressing a matter to many. While I believe that, in the language of Blaise Pascal, every human has a God-shaped void that only

God can fill, this sensitivity to God varies with individual humans, as do sensitivity to beauty or order or friendship. Thus, some persons may not be as burdened with a sense of sin or feel as grateful that their sins have been forgiven. Nor do many of us have these feelings with equal intensity at all times; I doubt that even the greatest saints have experienced such consistent longing or gratitude. It must have been in recognition of this spiritual ebb and flow that Charles Wesley prayed for "a sensibility of sin, / a pain to feel it near." And I suspect it is significant that he prayed, specifically, to feel "the first approach" of "pride or wrong desire." These sins are more subtle than the sins of outward conduct, or even the sins of the tongue, so a higher level of sensitivity is needed.

Even the best scholars can only speculate as to what drove the psalmist when he wrote our 103rd Psalm. Was it a particularly virulent act? It could be, but I think it could as easily have been simply a wandering of the will or a nurturing within the soul of feelings inconsistent with godliness. Whatever the sin, the writer now feels what a hymnist described in another generation as "the joy of sins forgiven, / the bliss the blood-washed know." He realizes that justice has not been done. He hasn't gotten what he deserves. "[God] does not deal with us according to our sins, / nor repay us according to our iniquities" (Ps. 103:10), and for that he is profoundly grateful. So grateful, in fact, that he has to resort to the largest metaphor available to us humans, "as the heavens are high above the earth."

Whatever the sin for which the poet has found forgiveness, I suspect it is something that has burdened his spirit for a long time. I judge this from the pleasure he feels in the degree of separation between himself and his transgressions. Perhaps, like Paul, he had found himself a "wretched man" who carried about a veritable "body of death" (Rom. 7:24). Now the psalmist rejoices that his transgressions are removed "as far as the east is from the west" (Ps. 103:12). Again, the poet struggles for an adequate metaphor; how can one expect any poor earthly language to convey so heavenly an experience?

In the New Testament, God is frequently portrayed as father, whether in the language of Jesus and Paul or in parabolic form, but rarely in the Old Testament. This Psalm is one of those rare instances, and it is the most dramatic of the lot. Again, one feels the psalmist is struggling for a metaphor that will carry the wonder of his experience. So he writes,

> As a father has compassion for his children,
>   so the LORD has compassion for those who fear him.
>   (Ps. 103:13)

The language is more daring in the Hebrew than in the English, because the Hebrew word translated "have compassion" is in the Hebrew customarily associated with motherly love, sometimes with a word like "fondle"; because the Hebrew word is from the same root as the word for "womb," which might well be considered the ultimate place of fondling, and thus of compassion. So the psalmist is not only comparing God's goodness to the gentle nature of an earthly father at his best, but more than that, for the feminine side of the earthly father.

And why is God so compassionate? Quite simply, because we need it.

> For he knows how we were made;
>   he remembers that we are dust.
>   (Ps. 103:14)

The compassion we receive is not a meritorious award; it is recognition of our helpless estate. We were made from the dust, and to the dust we return. Shakespeare puts our dust in context when in *Hamlet* he says, "Imperious Caesar, dead and turn'd to clay, / Might stop a hole to keep the wind away."[1] We may be noble creatures, only a little lower than the angels, but we are made of the most common stuff, and short of resurrection it is to such that we return. Which is to say, we need all the help we can get. So the Lord, plenteous in mercy, extends to us the kind of compassion a motherly father would give. And it is unearned. Like grace.

I said at the outset that I wish I knew the circumstances under which this psalm was written. On considered thought, I back away from that wish. Passing curiosity would like to know, but my better nature is satisfied to continue in ignorance. Perhaps, indeed, it is not my better nature; because what appeals to me so much about this psalm is that it *belongs* to me. As one of those souls who has failed so often to be what

I've dreamed of being and who has good reason for the place in the ritual that calls for the confession of sins, I know what it is to rejoice in God's forgiveness. And because I have a better than average memory for remembering my failures, I want especially to know God's goodness in removing those failures from my tenacious seeking.

When I think of such goodness, such compassion and mercy, I realize that it is altogether beyond my deserving. For whatever reason David or someone like him wrote this psalm so long ago, I am grateful. With childlike selfishness, I feel he wrote them also for me. They are words of grace, and I am grateful for them.

Chapter 17

Giving Grace a Name

Scripture Reading: The Prophet Hosea

*I*t is now seventy-five years since Marc Connelly's play, *Green Pastures*, opened on Broadway. I wish the production could be revived, though I understand why today it could be offensive to many. Connelly based the play on Roark Bradford's book, *Ol' Man Adam an' His Chillun*, giving a folk version of the Old Testament through the lives of the black community in the southern United States in the early part of the twentieth century. Near the end of the play, the Lord God comes to visit the camp of the people of Israel, to talk with their leader, Hezdrel. Hezdrel, however, doesn't know that he's talking with God. When God asks Hezdrel how he can be so brave in the face of nearly hopeless circumstances, Hezdrel answers that it's because he has faith in the "dear Lawd God." God, still in incognito form, raises a question for Hezdrel; how can he be so sure about God when God has abandoned everyone in their camp. Hezdrel answers with righteous anger, "Who say dat? Who dare say dat of de Lawd God of Hosea?"[1]

I see this scene as one of the great faith-portrayals of the secular stage. In a sense, Marc Connelly was an unlikely person to convey such a message. By the time he wrote *Green Pastures* he was famous for the comedies he and George S. Kaufman wrote together. They were part of the legendary Algonquin Round Table, where urbane sophistication ruled the day. Conversations at the Algonquin were not usually of a kind to produce grand declarations of faith. Of course I have no right to assume that everything a novelist or playwright says through his or her characters necessarily reflects the convictions of the author. Yet there's no denying that *Green Pastures* is a story of faith, particularly as the play comes to its final curtain. When I find such a quality in a play or a novel, I ask myself what was going on in the writer's soul. Sometimes, whether our theme is noble or ignoble, we find it easier to be honest when we're speaking in the third person.

In any event, I'm altogether sure the playwright was on target when he defended the character of God by identifying God with the prophet Hosea. Why, specifically, Hosea? Why not the Lord God of the psalmist, or of Isaiah, Moses, Jeremiah, or Amos? All of them give us admirable insights into the divine character. But admirable as they are, it seems to me that none of them can approach Hosea in picturing grace. This is because Hosea does not simply preach grace, he embodies it. Look at Hosea, and you have another name for grace.

The book of the prophet Hosea has a number of magnificent phrases and paragraphs, but the unique power of the book is in the story of the prophet himself. It is a strange, troubling story, not one for delicate tastes. One of the peculiarities of our time is that we are almost beyond shocking in secular matters, but painfully uneasy in matters religious. As the Bible tells the story, Hosea was a prophet in the land of Israel at a time when judgment was about to fall; the sins of the nation had brought it to a place of impending tragedy. Hosea tells us nothing about his age, his town, or his daily occupation. All we know about him is his marriage. This experience, and the love it embodies, becomes the loom on which God weaves a message to Israel.

"When the LORD first spoke through Hosea," it was to give him a command, reasonable enough in its basic declaration, but nearly indefensible in its particulars: "Go, take for yourself a wife" (Hos. 1:2). That's fine, except that this wife was to be "a wife of whoredom," who in turn would have "children of whoredom" (Hos. 1:2). Scholars differ as to whether Hosea's wife, Gomer, was a prostitute at the time of the marriage or whether the unfaithfulness came later. No matter; one way or the other, Hosea knew what he was getting into.

During the next several years, Hosea and Gomer had three children. In each instance, God asked that Hosea give the child a symbolic name. First, a boy named Jezreel; Jezreel was a city in Israel where Jehu had taken over the government a generation earlier, and the name was therefore symbolic of political power and activity. Then, a daughter named Lo-ruhamah, meaning "not pitied," because God would no longer have pity on the house of Israel or forgive them. The third child, another son, was named Lo-ammi, which meant, "not my people," because "you are not my people and I am not your God" (Hos. 1:9).

At this point I invite you to flesh out the story with me. I suspect that it was sometime not long after the birth of this third child that Hosea sensed something was happening to his marriage. Perhaps he felt a distance in his wife; not surprising, he may have reasoned, when she had had three children in rather a short period, and was preoccupied with their care. Perhaps Hosea noticed she was at the market or the town well longer than the errand normally required. He sensed some days that his village friends looked at him strangely, some becoming overly cordial, and others noticeably uneasy in his presence.

Then, one day, Gomer was gone. She disappeared from the area and from the lives of the family; disappeared so completely that she didn't bother even to inquire about her children. In time, word got back to Hosea: she was a prostitute now, moving from place to place, so cheap it was as if she despised herself. At home, with the awkward hands of a man, Hosea tried to care for the three children, hoping to give them a double portion of love while he groaned for his own destitution of love.

I think it was at such a time, one day when Hosea was—with reason—pitying himself and questioning the meaning of it all, that the Lord God came to him. "Hosea?"

"Yes, Lord."

"I know what you're going through."

Hosea wanted to be courteous and reverent, but how could God understand the kind of pain he was enduring?

"Hosea, I loved your people, Israel, and betrothed them to myself. I courted them in the howling wilderness and watched over them in Egypt. When they were ugly and unwashed, despised among the nations, I clasped them hard to myself. But they have left me, Hosea, the way Gomer has left you, and now they lie under every green tree with any lover.

"But I haven't given up. I will 'bring [Israel] into the wilderness, / and speak tenderly to her. . . . There she shall respond as in the days of her youth, / as at the time when she came out of the land of Egypt'" (Hos. 2:14, 16). "And this, Hosea, is how I want you to go after Gomer.

Hunt her out and bring her back to your house, to be your wife, and thus to be a living sign to Israel of my love for them."

So Hosea found Gomer at last, on the slave market; so useless now that he bought her for half the standard price of a slave, plus what was probably a day's ration of food. And they went home, to try again. Obviously, it was not going to be easy. There would be a long period of discipline and rebuilding, until at last there could be a solid, enduring relationship.

The Bible doesn't tell us how Hosea's marriage to Gomer finally turned out. For the rest of the book, the prophet devotes himself entirely to the anguish and struggle of God's love for the nation of Israel. That story, of course, has not come to an end. Many Christian commentators, beginning with St. Jerome (c. 347–420), have applied Hosea's story of God and Israel to God and the church. Which is to say—what Hosea experienced in his lifetime, God has experienced repeatedly over the centuries, not only with the chosen peoples as a whole, but with all of us who have identified ourselves individually as believers.

Some years ago a popular Christian writer, Philip Yancey, realized that his beliefs about the Bible and its teachings were largely a product of things others had told him, whether in sermons, classes, or books. He wondered how the Bible would sound to him if he were to read it without any outside helps and opinions. So he settled into a Colorado mountain cabin for two winter weeks, to read his Bible from Genesis to its end. As he came to the end of his intensive reading, he concluded that the Bible is not so much a collection of decrees, nor a description of the divine attributes. Above all else, he said, the Bible is the story of God "the Jilted Lover."[2] I read Yancey's insight with full agreement. My own reading of the Bible over the years had led me to the same conclusion, if not perhaps in as descriptive language.

It's an unlikely picture of God, is it not? To be God is to be in control, not to be susceptible to the whims of others. God, one thinks, should give commands, not solicit favor or affection. A solicitous God is almost a blasphemy, or at the least, an embarrassment. Yet this is the picture of God that emerges all through the Bible. This may help us understand some of the dramatic language of the Old Testament, where we're told that God is a "jealous God," and where some of the divine activity seems quite petty. The Old Testament writers are never cautious about showing God in such light; it as if they took for granted (and expected us to do the same) that when one loves intensely, one sometimes does foolish things, the sort of things that can't be explained except by saying, "That's the way it is when you love."

During the period when Marc Connelly's *Green Pastures* was on Broadway, a New York playwright who identified himself pseudonymously as Izachak published a three-act play that he titled *The Marriage of Hosea*. His subtitle was *A passion play*. It was the finest kind of double entendre, for those who dare to see the connection between passion as they usually understand it in romantic love but as expressed ultimately in God's reach for our human race—and still more, of course, from a Christian vantage point, where we refer to the sufferings of our Lord as his "passion."

This picture of God's love for our human race and of the continuing divine pursuit is the consistent theme of the Old Testament. The unfolding of that theme sometimes travels through unlikely terrain, but the basic point is unchanged. All the way from the Garden of Eden through the history of Israel and the pronouncements of the prophets there is the insistence that God wants a voluntary response from us humans. God, being God, could surely have programmed us so that we would always do the right thing, with the computer of our brains set so that our only inclination would be to fulfill the divine will. Instead, biblical theology teaches, God created us free moral agents, able to love God or to ignore him, able to follow like saints or wander into any dissolute and destructive path.

How does God respond to all of this? As the book of Hosea draws near its end, God reminds Hosea of the love with which he has pursued Israel. "When Israel was a child, I loved him, / and out of Egypt I called my son." Unfortunately, "[t]he more I called them, / the more they went from me" (Hos. 11:1–2). God's pathos increases. "It was I who taught Ephraim [Israel] to walk, / . . . but they did not know that I healed them. / I led them with cords of human kindness, / with bands of love. . . . I bent down to them and fed them" (Hos. 11:3–4). This is the language of a rejected suitor, or a parent who can't understand why a child would so indifferently and insolently turn away. It is pathetic language, the sort you've heard from a friend or neighbor whose love has been betrayed. "How could he do this to me?" It isn't language for a God, is it? But Hosea is not done. Now the prophet, still speaking for God, cries out in what seem like racking sobs, "How can I give you up, Ephraim? / How can I hand you over, O Israel?" (Hos. 11:8).

By definition, God should have the right to be imperious. Instead, the Bible portrays God's humility. Mind you, there are times when the biblical writers speak of the grandeur of God, and times when they picture God as self-asserting and demanding of divine rights. But these portrayals only make more dramatic the picture of God as suppliant, holy hat in hand, seeking the favor of an arrogant creation and of us arrogant members of the creation. If we were not at times reminded of the rights of God we would have no basis for understanding the divine humility.

In Connelly's play, God—incognito—continues to challenge the faithful, trusting Hezdrel, until at last God announces that he's about to go, and asks if Hezdrel has any message that should be taken to the people. Hezdrel answers, "Tell de people in de hills dey ain't nobody like de Lawd God of Hosea."[3]

Hezdrel has it right; there's no one like the Lord God of Hosea. This is a God who follows errant humanity down the unfaithfulness of our backslidings, through the alleys and back streets and escape patterns of life, even to the slave markets into which we humans sell ourselves. And let it be said, lest we see ourselves with jaundiced eyes, that a slave is a slave, whether in the addicts' recovery ward or in the distracting loveliness of the concert hall. Only the setting is changed, to deflect our egos. Wherever and whatever, God will pursue us and seek to bring us back. This is love quite beyond logic, beyond good sense or even good taste. But after all, whoever expected love to be marked by good taste?

Call it grace. And in the Old Testament, call it *Hosea*.

Chapter 18

The Old Testament Synonym for Grace

Scripture Lesson: Several Old Testament passages

*T*he best evidence that we are social creatures may be the way memory hangs its data on persons. Places and occasions are important, too, but persons lead the way. We remember a song because of the person with whom we first heard it; a book because of the person who told us about it; a restaurant because of the person or persons with whom we ate there. For a sports fan, a baseball or football game stands in its own right, but we don't go far into reporting its high moments without mentioning the person who was with us. Several years ago, I went alone to a church service in Washington, DC, but I still remember the man who sat next to me in the pew.

I first met the Hebrew word *hesed* during my seminary education, and because I love the Psalms, I had pursued it a bit in private study. But I remember the day it became special to me, and the person who made it so. I was bringing Rabbi Manfred Swarsensky from the Cleveland, Ohio, airport to the Church of the Saviour, where that evening he would speak to my congregation. As we drove on the interstate above an area marked by the onion-domed churches of the Eastern Orthodox immigrants who had come to that area generations before to man the steel industry, and some of whose descendants still lived there, Manfred was telling me about *hesed*. "There is a Hebrew word that is very special. There is no single word that will translate it into English. Even a paragraph will hardly do. This is *hesed*."

The churches and the ethnic neighborhood to which I have referred had nothing to do with our conversation. I refer to them only because the experience was all of a piece. It was a sacred moment for me, still vivid in my mind two decades later. During the ten years that I was a pastor in Madison, Wisconsin, Manfred Swarsensky was one of my two most cherished clergy colleagues. I'm sure I never told him that; perhaps I didn't fully realize it then.

His comments about *hesed* stayed with me because I knew, even as he spoke, that he had more right to the word than I did. Because of his Jewish descent, he owned the word, and because of his lifelong knowledge of Hebrew he understood its derivations; but beyond all of that, my friend owned the word because he had bought it by his life experience.

Manfred Swarsensky was a rabbi in Berlin when Adolf Hitler came to power. He was a person of great influence within the Jewish community, and was therefore a marked person. In time he was arrested and put into prison. His doom was certain, but somehow he escaped; he never said how. I only know that some forty years later, the mayor of Berlin brought him back to the city as an honored guest. In the meanwhile, he had come to America as an immigrant, had served as rabbi of a new congregation in Madison, Wisconsin, Temple Beth-El, and in the passage of time had become probably the most respected citizen of that university community. Manfred Swarsensky knew something about *hesed*.

Hesed, as we have already said, is difficult if not impossible to translate into English. Mary Ellen Chase, a legendary teacher for a generation of students at Smith College in the mid-twentieth century, said that the "most outstanding characteristic of God in the words and thoughts of the psalmists" was this Hebrew word. The translation she liked best was *loving-kindness*, a word Miles Coverdale, the sixteenth-century bishop and Bible translator, developed to fill a gap in English as he went about his translating. Dr. Chase liked *loving-kindness* for its "more personal connotation." Much as I like the work of Coverdale and William Tyndale, I would also cast a vote for the term that appears often in several modern versions, including the New Revised Standard Version, "steadfast love." But Chase continued that *hesed* "surely contains the suggestion of *compassion*, and even of *companionship*. Perhaps this last-named quality, *companionship,* is the most inherent element in *lovingkindness* since the Hebrew word *chesedh* is inseparable from the sense of a *covenant*, an *agreement*, an *understanding* between God and man." With it all, Dr. Chase continued, there was always the idea of God's "active participation" in our daily affairs.[1]

I realize that perceptions tend to reflect the eye of the beholder, but let me venture an opinion. I submit that three words constitute the continuing theme of the Old Testament, the motifs around which all the other submelodies play: holiness, justice, and *hesed*. God's holiness is the foundation of the Old Testament law; Israel was commanded to be holy because God was holy. There was finality to this argument; the God with whom they were doing business was holy, so holiness was expected of them. Justice, too, was a prime characteristic of God, so the people of Israel were to "love justice," because God was just. There is a stark, dramatic beauty in holiness and justice; one admires these qualities, but at a distance. *Hesed*, however, embraces us. Its profile is accepting, its beauty is warm. God's holiness and justice evoke my admiration, my reverence, and my desire to be a better person than I am; God's *hesed* evokes my love.

This word appears all through the Old Testament story. When Lot pleads with the angelic visitors for a better destination as he leaves Sodom, he confesses that already he has received *hesed* so he is properly apologetic in asking for more (Gen. 19:19). When Moses leads the people in thanks to God following their escape from Egypt, he recalls that it was in *hesed* that God had "led the people whom you redeemed" (Exod. 15:13). In the commandment forbidding idols, the people are reminded that God shows *hesed* "to the thousandth generation of those who love me and keep my commandments" (Exod. 20:6), a vow that God repeats as Moses gets replacement tablets of the law after Israel's sin at Sinai (Exod. 34:7). Generations later, as the Ark of the Covenant is brought into Solomon's temple, the Levitical singers, "with trumpets and cymbals and other musical instruments" praise God with the song,

> For he is good,
> for his [*hesed*] endures forever.
> (2 Chr. 5:13)

Many generations and many kings later, after the nation had wandered so far from God that it had divided into two bodies, Israel and Judah, and the northern portion (Israel) had disappeared into the surrounding nations, Judah—all that was left—was taken captive by the Babylonians and then the Persians. It looked as if the dream was utterly gone; the diminished nation was now in captivity, right back where they were so many generations earlier when God had sent Moses to deliver them. It was a bad scene, a quite pathetic one. But two remarkable men, Ezra and Nehemiah, helped the scattered remnants of the people to rebuild their cherished capital, Jerusalem. In a day of national confession, Ezra prayed for the people. They were being restored, Ezra said, because God was "gracious and merciful, slow to anger and abounding in *hesed*" (Neh. 9:17). This covenant love could not be broken even by the continued intransigence of the nation.

The prophets loved this word, too. Jeremiah, who is remembered more for his laments than for songs of victory, receives assurance from God and passes it on to the people. The streets of Jerusalem and Judah that are forsaken will one day hear again "the voice of mirth and the voice of gladness, the voice of the bridegroom and the voice of the bride"; and when they do, the song will be a familiar one:

> Give thanks to the LORD of hosts,
>   for the LORD is good,
>   for his *hesed* endures forever!
>   (Jer. 33:11)

Hosea uses *hesed* as part of his appeal for righteousness, promising the people that if they will sow for themselves "righteousness," they will "reap *hesed*."

But it is in the Psalms that *hesed* comes most abundantly into its own. The word appears over one hundred times in the Psalter. But of course we would expect as much. The Psalms are an expression of the soul, and no word carries more quality of soul than the word *hesed*. I see the book of Psalms as the supreme expression of the divine-human friendship. The writers are so confident that God understands them that they dare to speak their mind to God even when one thinks they might better keep their thoughts to themselves. One has to be very confident of a friendship to speak as candidly to anyone as the psalmists speak to God.

This perception of an unfailing friendship springs naturally from the mood that *hesed* developed in the soul. As Nelson Glueck put it,

"Thus *hesed* can be translated as 'loyalty' and also as 'love' so as to emphasize that it is Yahweh's hesed. However, one must remain aware that a very particular kind of 'love' is meant, conforming to loyalty and obligation and thereby fulfilling the conditions of the covenant."[2] If one believes that God is utterly loyal, and that this loyalty is one guaranteed by a covenant, one can feel sublime confidence; and all the more so when this covenant loyalty is ensconced in love. If the loyalty were only a contractual relationship, it would be assuring, but when the relationship is also structured with love, the confidence is beyond reason or argument. Such is the quality of *hesed* as it appears again and again in the book of Psalms. The covenant is sure, the friendship is secure, the love is unfailing. No wonder, then, that the poet declared *hesed* "better than life" (Ps. 63:3). Some things, if taken from life, leave life's value so diminished that its very definition is changed.

Like grace, *hesed* is appreciated most when it is needed most. If we were closer to the saintliness that is the goal of God's people, we would be grateful for the gentleness and generosity of God's character in the midst of our abundance and our victories, but generally our sensitivity is dulled by prosperity, and we gain perspective at the edges of despair. So it was with the psalmists. The writer may declare, "For your *hesed* is as high as the heavens" (Ps. 57:10), but he has come to that conclusion after a period of "destroying storms," and experiences with those who "trample on" him, and who "set a net for my steps" and "a pit in my path." It is through such near despair that the wonder of *hesed* revealed itself most fully.

Nelson Glueck adds to our understanding. "The longing for God's *hesed* by the pious is not to be explained by their understandable wish to be delivered out of their straits but, foremost, because deliverance through *hesed* would give them assurance of being in a covenantal relationship with God. They believed in His *hesed* even when their actual fate sometimes brought them close to despair. For them, the most precious thing in life, and an end in itself, was the covenantal relationship to God which was manifested by *hesed*."[3]

This passion for the covenant relationship showed itself, in some instances, in challenging God. In a time of great trial the poet fears that the Lord might "never again be favorable." And what, above all else, is at issue? "Has his *hesed* ceased forever? / Are his promises at an end for all time?" (Ps. 77:8). The poet is asking a rhetorical question, but he expects his answer to come, not from some human listener, but from God. In another instance, the poet reasons with God: You had better deliver me in your *hesed*, because "in death there is no remembrance of you; / in Sheol who can give you praise?" (Ps. 6:5). The poet stands before God like a bargaining customer in a Middle Eastern bazaar: "What gain will you have in my loss?"

The other situation in which the cry for *hesed* is most poignant is at the time of transgression. The gods of neighboring nations showed little concern for moral conduct; not so with the God of Israel. As I said earlier, the quality of holiness is a supreme issue in biblical faith. And because God is holy, God does not wink at the sins of those who claim relationship with him. So the psalmist cries, in one of the Songs of Ascents,

> If you, O LORD, should mark iniquities,
> Lord, who could stand?

And then he encourages his soul: "But there is forgiveness with you, / so that you may be revered" (Ps. 130:3–4). But as the writer waits for God, he does so with hope for covenantal mercy. It is interesting, too, to see how easily the prayer of the psalmist moves between the personal and the national. "My soul waits for the Lord," but it is Israel as well that needs redemption from "all its iniquities."

> O Israel, hope in the LORD!
>> For with the LORD there is *hesed*,
>> and with him is great power to redeem.
> It is he who will redeem Israel
>> from all its iniquities.
>
> (Ps. 130:7–8)

Psalm 90 makes only one reference to the sins of the writer and his associates; the primary emphasis is on our human frailty as compared to God's eternal power. But of course our sins demonstrate our frailty; if we were truly strong, we would also be holy. The writer speaks especially of those matters that only God can see: "You have set our iniquities before you, / our secret sins in the light of your countenance"

(Ps. 90:8). We can't help noting that the sins we thought "secret" are not hidden from the "light" of God's countenance. So it is with all of this that the writer pleads, "Turn, O LORD! How long? / Have compassion on your servants! / Satisfy us in the morning with your *hesed*, / so that we may rejoice and be glad all our days" (Psalm 90:13–14).

Perhaps it is particularly because of the way *hesed* is used in the book of Psalms that Norman Snaith defined the word as "the steady, persistent refusal of God to wash his hands of wayward Israel."[4] If Snaith's somewhat whimsical observation is correct—and it's easy to make a case for it—then all of us later sinners would add, "And I, also."

Certainly *hesed* demonstrates that, to use a common phrase, there is nothing in our badness that is too much for God's goodness. So it is that the Old Testament writers—prophets, poets, persons of wisdom—took hold of the strength they found in *hesed*. Were they in need? Here was hope. Had they embarrassed themselves by transgression? *Hesed* promised a God who could separate them from their sins. Were their enemies powerful beyond their resources? Turn, then, to a God who will not fail the covenant. Does everything seem lost, so that nothing awaits but the pit? Argue, then, with God on the basis of God's *hesed*. It is a word for all seasons in our frail, irregular, inconsistent human journey.

Soon after I became the minister at the First United Methodist Church in Madison, Wisconsin, Eve Brewster came to visit me. She had been a missionary in the Far East, and was a woman of high intelligence and transparent goodness. In the course of offering some insights about the church and community to which I had just come, she said, "I hope you will soon meet Rabbi Manfred Swarsensky. He is probably the finest Christian in our city." I was troubled by her statement, partly because I didn't think a faithful Jew would wish to be classified as a Christian, and partly because of the theological problems in her statement.

As time went by, I realized that Eve knew what she was saying. Hers was not a theological statement, but a witness to a person's character, as viewed from a Christian's standards. And as time went by, I knew why she said what she did. Her remarks came back to me, some fifteen years later, as Manfred and I drove from the Cleveland airport to the Church of the Saviour. I knew why he loved *hesed.* He had clung to it through the indignities of the early days of the Nazi rule, then through imprisonment that was expected to end in execution. It had sustained him through his escape and his flight to America, and then through the years of mastering a new language in a new world, while building a new congregation in a demanding city. And especially, because—true to the Old Testament teaching—he extended to others the *hesed* that God had extended to him.

Hesed is not the same as grace; theologians and students of Hebrew and Greek will point out differences. But *hesed* is near enough kin to remind us that God did not discover grace at the cross. The unfailing, unfathomable goodness of God began before the creation. It is part of the very nature of God. Without it, we humans would find our planet uninhabitable.

Notes

CHAPTER 1: GRACE IN THE MORNING

1. *The Pentateuch and Haftorahs*, 2nd ed., edited by J. H. Hertz (London: Soncino Press, 1967), 2.
2. Everett Fox, *The Five Books of Moses* (New York: Schocken Books, 1995), 17.
3. Hertz, 195.
4. Eleanor Farjeon, "Morning Has Broken," *The Presbyterian Hymnal* (Louisville, KY: Westminster/John Knox Press, 1990), #469.

CHAPTER 3: THE MAN WHO REFUSED GRACE

1. Everett Fox, *The Five Books of Moses* (New York: Schocken Books, 1995), 25.
2. Julia H. Johnston, "Grace Greater than Our Sin," *United Methodist Hymnal* (Nashville: United Methodist Publishing House, 1989), #365.
3. Fox, 27.

CHAPTER 4: GRACE IN A BROTHER'S FACE

1. Everett Fox, *The Five Books of Moses* (New York: Schocken Books, 1995), xi.
2. Ibid., xii.
3. Ibid., xii.

CHAPTER 5: GRACE IN A HARLOT'S TENT

1. Edwin C. Goldberg, *Midrash for Beginners* (Northvale, NJ: Jason Aronson Inc., 1996), 19, 20. The quotation from Rabbi Samuel ben Nahman is from *Genesis Rabbah*, 85:1.
2. Simone Weil, *Waiting for God*, trans. Emma Craufured (New York: Harper & Row, 1973), 48–49.

CHAPTER 6: GRACE ONCE A WEEK

1. Benno Jacob, "The Decalogue," *Jewish Quarterly Review*, 1923, xiv, 165; quoted in Joseph L. Baron, ed., *A Treasury of Jewish Quotations* (South Brunswick, NJ: A. S. Barnes and Co. Inc., 1965), 428.

2. Hermann Cohen, *Die Religion der Vernunft*, 540, 184; quoted in Baron, *Treasury of Jewish Quotations*.

3. Thomas Cahill, *The Gifts of the Jews* (New York: Nan A. Talese Doubleday, 1998), 144–45.

4. Jean Rhys, *Voyage in the Dark*; quoted in Elizabeth Knowles, *Oxford Dictionary of Quotations* (New York: Oxford University Press, 1999), 625.

CHAPTER 7: GRACIOUS COMMANDMENTS

1. Thomas Cahill, *The Gift of the Jews* (New York: Nan A. Talese Doubleday, 1998), 140.

2. Ibid., 142.

3. Dorothy L. Sayers, *Creed or Chaos* (Manchester, NH: Sophia Instituto Press, 1999), 73.

CHAPTER 8: GOD'S UNLIKELY CHOICES

1. J. Clinton McCann, "Choose, Chosen, Elect, Election," in Donald E. Gowan, ed., *The Westminster Theological Wordbook of the Bible* (Louisville, KY: Westminster John Knox Press, 2003), 56.

2. Quoted in Justin Kaplan, gen. ed., *Bartlett's Familiar Quotations*, 17th ed., (Boston: Little, Brown and Company, 2002), 706fn. (For those unfamiliar with Yiddish, "Goyim" refers to all non-Jews.)

CHAPTER 9: ONE MORE GRAND CHANCE

1. David Rosenberg, ed., *Congregation* (New York: Harcourt Brace Jovanovich, Publishers, 1987), 85.

2. Leo Rosten, *The Joys of Yiddish* (New York: Pocket Books, 1970), 348–50.

3. Franz Wright, "Letter," quoted in *Arkansas Democrat-Gazette*, April 24, 2004, 4B.

CHAPTER 12: NEW EVERY MORNING

1. Arthur John Gossip, "But When Life Tumbles In, What Then?" in Clyde E. Fant Jr. and William M. Pinson Jr., eds., *20 Centuries of Great Preaching*, vol. 8 (Waco, TX: Word Books, 1971), 235.

CHAPTER 14: INDOMITABLE GRACE

1. Robert Gordis, *The Book of God and Man* (Chicago: University of Chicago Press, 1965), 3.

2. Archibald MacLeish, *J.B.* (Boston: Houghton Mifflin Company, 1956, 1958), 11.

CHAPTER 15: SONGS OF DIS-GRACE

1. William Shakespeare, *Sonnet 29.*
2. Mary Ellen Chase, *The Psalms for the Common Reader* (New York: W. W. Norton & Company, 1962), 81.

CHAPTER 16: BETTER THAN WE CAN EVER DESERVE

1. William Shakespeare, *Hamlet*, V, i, 235.

CHAPTER 17: GIVING GRACE A NAME

1. Marc Connelly, *The Green Pastures* (London: Delisle, 1963), 85.
2. Philip Yancey, "God, the Jilted Lover," *Christianity Today*, May 16, 1986, 72.
3. Connelly, *Green Pastures*, 87.

CHAPTER 18: THE OLD TESTAMENT SYNONYM FOR GRACE

1. Mary Ellen Chase, *The Psalms for the Common Reader* (New York: W. W. Norton, 1962), 88–89.
2. Nelson Glueck, Hesed *in the Bible* (Cincinnati: Hebrew Union College Press, 1967), 73.
3. Ibid., 92.
4. Norman H. Snaith, "Loving-kindness" in *A Theological Word Book of the Bible,* ed. Alan Richardson (New York: Macmillan, 1951), 136–37, quoted in Glueck, Hesed *in the Bible*, 9.